MAGICAL URBANISM

La Mona. Photograph by Alessandra Moctezuma

MAGICAL URBANISM

Latinos Reinvent the US City

───────◆───────

MIKE DAVIS

VERSO

London · New York

A HAYMARKET BOOK

First published by Verso 2000
© Mike Davis 2000
All rights reserved

VERSO
UK: 6 Meard Street, London W1V 3 HR
US: 180 Varick Street, 10th Floor, New York, NY 10014-4606

VERSO is the imprint of New Left Books

ISBN 1 85984 771 4

British Library Cataloguing in Publication Data
A catalogue record for this book is available from the British Library

Library of Congress Cataloging-in-Publication Data
A catalog record for this book is available from the Library of Congress

Typeset in Dante by Steven Hiatt, San Francisco
Printed and bound in the USA by R.R. Donnelly & Sons Co.

Dedicated to the memory of
Roberto Naduris (1946–1995):

"Compañero, your smile lives on in our hearts"

CONTENTS

When you say "America" you refer to the territory
stretching between the icecaps of the two poles. So to hell with
your barriers and frontier guards!

Diego Rivera, San Francisco 1931

Foreword

LATINOS AND THE
CROSSOVER AESTHETIC

Román de la Campa

It is often said that globalization moves the world past nationalist
zealousness, though there is growing evidence that globalization
may also embolden it. The push towards utopias without borders
such as trade free zones, transnational currencies, nomadic workfor-
ces and the ever-expansive territory of the Internet may have brought
a new identity crisis to much of the world. Even rich, secure nations
like the United States have responded to these pressures with a wave
of protectionism as well as new laws regarding language use and
citizen rights. In this path-breaking book, Mike Davis looks at one of
the most important registers of the global epoch in the United States:
The Latino demographic growth, its ongoing impact on the design
of major American cities, its potential for social and political change
and its new claim on the American imaginary.

Latinos, Latin Americans, immigrants, exiles, refugees, border
peoples, rafters – it's becoming difficult to define the legal or

ontological status of this fluid diaspora of 32 million people in the United States. Yet they now constitute a growing political and economic force that can no longer be ignored. Davis's *Magical Urbanism* charts an inventive and well-researched guide through this momentous topic. What I'd like to do here, briefly, is to underline the issue of language and cultural dispersal as it pertains to Latinos. The topic of identity always calls for moments of intense reflection. One of mine came as I watched *West Side Story* one summer night in Miami many years ago. I asked myself why Puerto Ricans, whose presence in New York had a long history, were portrayed in such a negative light. I also wondered if other groups or individuals from the Caribbean – myself, for example – would be seen in a similar way. I was shaken a bit. Could one be an American and yet retain cultural, ethnic and linguistic differences without becoming a second-class citizen? Or was this just a problem for New York Puerto Ricans, whose class and racial background was generally different from that first migration wave of Cubans that brought me here? Later, as my stay grew longer and my own condition became a question, I discovered a more forgiving, but still stereotyped, image of someone of Latin background, in this case Cuban-born, who lived in the Unites States: Desi Arnaz's "latinity" often highlighted in *I Love Lucy*, focused on his Latin-lover looks (dark-but-still-within whiteness), accent and musical nature. At the time I also hadn't the slightest idea of what a Chicano might be or what the complex history between the United States and Mexico could portend. Cubans generally knew little about the rest of Latin America, and my years in the Midwest had taught me even less about it.

All Latinos in the United States can be said to share some characteristics besides the imposed need to identify ourselves with names we may not like or agree with, like Hispanic, Latino or hyphenated American. Even Cubans who stay within the boundaries of a closed, mostly Spanish-speaking community in Miami ultimately find their children or younger relatives immersed in the cultural realities of the United States and thus somewhat distanced from the nationalistic exile fervor of their elders. Some even seek, or are driven to, greater assimilation in the US mainstream, while many retain a plural disposition about language, culture and identity, like most other Latinos in the United States, whose points of origin have multiplied tremendously in the last two decades to include Dominicans, Colombians, Ecuadorians, Nicaraguans and Salvadoreans, among others. But this phenomenon is not limited to Latinos. New ethnic enclaves in the United States (Asian, West Indian, as well as Hispanic and/or Latino), made up of refugees, exiles, legal and illegal immigrants, boat people, rafters and tourists, defy categories that have been rendered meaningless by hemispheric migratory pressures. The Latino in the US is, therefore, a particular distraction to both myths, the "American melting-pot" concept modeled on white European experience, and the "Cuban exile" ideology of national reconquest, paradoxically (but perhaps only) kept alive by an intractable split between an aging *caudillo* in Cuba and a transplanted ruling class that has thrived economically in the United States.

The languages of social science run into uncharted territory when attempting to account for the post-melting-pot period of American history. Each Latino group may be unique, but even those that are newly arrived come to share a call for a different, if unstable, sense of ontological space characterized by a doubleness – too American to seriously undertake a return to the motherland, but able to nurture a different cultural and linguistic heritage in the United States, with which it maintains contact in multiple and contradictory ways. In the case of historically Latino groups such as Chicanos and Nuyoricans, it is not a question of returning anywhere, but of claiming, or retaining, a space of difference within the Americas, the United States as well as Latin America.

In this book, Mike Davis distinctly exemplifies many of the Latino and border zone shifts that are changing the way we understand the North/South divide and reshaping the Americas. My own experience suggests that the distance between "Latinos" and immigrant groups of Latin Americans who see themselves strictly as exiles and foreign nationals is also giving way to a fusion of considerable significance to both groups. It is worth repeating that it was only here in the United States that many native Cubans like myself actually met Latin Americans from many different countries, as the political and economic upheavals affecting their respective native lands brought us to the US in exile during the past thirty years or so. The same goes for other Latin Americans. It is also here where Latin Americans become part of the Latino population, particularly once we stray from our neighborhoods and families. At that point our experience, regardless of class and ethnicity, begins to acquire a sense of plurality deriving from a dual linguistic and cultural bearing.

Does the growing Latino or Hispanic population constitute a

potential political force, or should it be seen mainly as a nimble source of identity whose meaning remains in a state of contradictory flux? There is no pan-ethnic Latino identity as such, and national origin will always remain crucial in any grouping of this so-called "minority." But its presence as an identifiable entity in the United States does emerge in certain contexts, when its intrinsic diversity is fused together as a differential "other." This may be best understood in reference to Latin America itself, so diverse as to defy any sense of ethnic, linguistic or cultural whole. Yet, like Latinos in the United States, Latin America is often forced into a conceptual or political unity as a hemispheric or civilizational "other" to the United States, in a way that Canada, for example, generally is not (although that may be changing). Ironically, the constant influx of Latin Americans migrating to the United States has been shown to revitalize the Hispanic roots of Latinos in the US, thereby augmenting the distress felt by those who sense that this country is in danger of complicating its own identity.

The idea of the Latino is quite fertile precisely because it is problematic. It complicates how Latin Americans think of themselves now that constant migration between American border zones makes it hard to demarcate between Latinos and Latin America. So much contemporary television shown in Latin America is filmed in the United States and carries a Latino sensitivity, particularly the news shows, but also some hybrid shows like *Primer Impacto*, as well as the blither variety programs like *Cristina* and *Sábado Gigante*. Conversely, the influx of Latin Americans to the United States affects historical Latino groups, inching them closer to national roots and requiring greater levels of Span-

ish competence. The crossover effect is not only in the direction
of English, it also requires the capacity to get back into the Spanish markets, symbols and signs. This is the insight that guides the
current marketing of Latino music in the United States. It may
also be the insight that Richard Rodríguez lacked in his widely
read *Hunger of Memory*. His sense of rebirth through English and
melting-pot Americanism allowed him to leave behind a world of
Spanish he identified with a static paternal influence. But Rodríguez was too bound to his childhood traumas in that book to
recognize the growing importance of Spanish language and culture in the United States in the 1980s and 1990s. He failed to grasp
the crossover insight that came with the times – the thought that
he can love, and perform, in more than one language, or nation,
for that matter.

Rodríguez's second book of memoirs, *Days of Obligation*,
charts a different route on the interrelationship between language, literature and national identity. Though it is still somewhat
influenced by the author's need to punish Chicano ethnic politics,
he lets it be known, playfully, that he needs to learn a lot more
about Mexico, as well as Latin America and other related topics
that he is now being paid to write about by credit card companies,
magazines and other enterprises that are active agents in the constantly changing nature of the American character. His second
memoir can thus be read as a rather coy critique of his first. It
remains to be seen if *Days of Obligation* finds as many fervent
readers in high school and college English departments as *Hunger
of Memory*, but it certainly charts new paths for the author. The
result is a highly ironic and wickedly equivocal attempt to write in

English about contemporary Latin America and Latino-California themes. One can't help but notice that a crossover aesthetic has found its way to Richard Rodríguez, and he in turn seems to have discovered a new America in which he can be a Latino writer after all. I'm inclined to believe the literary dash of his second book seduced the ethnic fears of his first.

The renowned Mexican poet-philosopher Octavio Paz, a cultural icon for generations of Latin American poets and writers far removed from any Latino sensitivities, once came across a group of *Pachucos* while strolling through the city of Los Angeles in the mid 1940s. He had never seen or heard about them, but he was suddenly struck by the realization they had something to do with him. As told in his *Labyrinth of Solitude*, Paz was dumbfounded upon discovering that a Latin American's inward gaze must necessarily incorporate the contradictory insights that await him or her in the Latino population of the United States.

The same potential for crossover insights can be found in the relationship between Latinos and Americans. Latinos are without a doubt the most profound challenge to the American melting pot myth, in that they don't adhere to just English, or to the one-drop definition of racial Otherness, and they are themselves part of an American migration with a rich history in this Hemisphere. It is often asked why Latinos don't simply conform to established forms of assimilation to American life. One answer might be that Latinos are already deeply American, they derive from a North/South divide that is yielding a new geography, and they are thoroughly engaged in the project of further defining what Americanness means.

Stumbling into one's double is always a startling but telling experience. It happened to Paz in a city whose rich Mexican heritage should not have been a surprise to him. For Richard Rodríguez, it was an image conjured up by a literary market whose demand for Latino themes he could no longer disdain. There is an interesting lesson in both cases. The study of Latinos can only begin by charting unsuspected encounters, with full awareness that the task is bound to find unsuspected mirrors bound to reflect the researcher's unguarded gaze. Topics such as these demand an ear for artistic flows as well as a deep understanding of political and economic forces that are shaping our landscape. Readers of *Magical Urbanism* will find a unique attempt to engage these challenges.

1

SPICING THE CITY

Sometime during 1996, at the very latest, Latinos surpassed African-Americans as the second largest ethno-racial group in New York City. (They had long been the largest census group in the Bronx.) There were no street celebrations in El Barrio or Quisqueya (Washington Heights), nor did the mayor hold a press conference from the steps of Gracie Mansion. Indeed, most New Yorkers were oblivious to this demographic watershed, which was first announced in an academic working paper.[1] Yet it was an epochal event all the same: comparable to the numerical ascendance of the Irish during the 1860s or the peaking of Black migration to New York City a century later. Thanks to a booming Spanish-surname population, no borough except Staten Island any longer has a majority ethnicity.

Four years later California celebrated the millennium as the second mainland state (after New Mexico) to become a "majority-minority" society. Dramatically ahead of earlier projections, white non-Hispanics (nearly 80 percent of the population in 1970) became a minority for the first time since the Gold Rush.[2] Without discounting the cultural and economic dynamism of recent Asian immigration, the major engine of this stunning metamorphosis has been the Mexicanization of Southern California.[3] At the beginning of the Vietnam War, Los Angeles still had the highest percentage of native-born white Protestants of the ten biggest US cities. But Latinos moved into the passing lane in the late 1970s when they achieved a plurality in the City of Los Angeles: by 1998 they outnumbered Anglos in Los Angeles County by more than a million. Within forty years, moreover, an estimated 13–15 million Latinos will be the majority everywhere south of the Tehachapis.[4]

New York and Los Angeles are, respectively, the second and third largest metropolitan economies on earth (Tokyo-Yokohama is the largest), and their ethnic transformation mirrors a decisive national trend with important international resonances.[5] Salsa is becoming the predominant ethnic flavor – and rhythm – in major US metropolitan areas. In six of the ten biggest cities – New York, Los Angeles, Houston, San Diego, Phoenix and San Antonio, in that order – Latinos now outnumber Blacks; and in Los Angeles, Houston and San Antonio, non-Hispanic whites as well. Within a few years, both Dallas and Fort Worth will have Spanish-surname pluralities, while in Chicago Latinos are now 27 percent of the population and hold the balance of power in most city elections.[6] Indeed, as Illinois' Latino population (mainly in Chicago and its inner suburbs) nearly doubles by 2020, they will become the state's largest minority.[7] Philadelphia's Latinos – traditional

"Philaricans" as well as more recent Colombian and Central
American immigrants – will remain a second-place minority for
the foreseeable future, but they have provided most of the city's
demographic energy over the last decade, boosting themselves
from 6 percent of the population in 1990 to more than 10 percent
in 2000.[8] Likewise, metro Boston now has Latino-majority suburbs like Lawrence (and soon Chelsea), while the low-paid service
working class of the Beltway (like the District of Columbia itself)
is increasingly Salvadorean or Mexican. Only Detroit, with the
most threadbare private-sector economy of any major central
city, clearly stands apart from the trend. (On the other hand, Latinos have been the fastest growing population group in Michigan
as a whole and now comprise more than 10 percent of the population of small cities and towns like Saginaw, Adrian and Shelby.)[9]

   In the broader census universe, eighteen of the twenty-five
most populous US counties (good statistical surrogates for metropolitan cores) will have larger Latino than Black populations by
2003.[10] Although urban centers where Latinos are majorities or
the largest minority are still concentrated in the southwestern tier
of states, Spanish-surname populations have also been growing in
hothouse fashion in cities with negligible historical Mexican or
Spanish connections like Anchorage (20,000), Portland (115,000),
Salt Lake City (40 percent of the elementary school population)
and Milwaukee (100,000).[11] Regionally, both the Pacific Northwest and New England now have larger Spanish-surname than
Black populations, and Latinos provided an incredible 50 percent
of population growth in ten Central states over the last generation – thus sparking debate on the "Browning of the Midwest."[12]

A decade ago Latinos were a negligible element in the cultural landscape of the New South. Exponential growth of the Latino population in the 1990s (149 percent in Arkansas, 110 percent in North Carolina, 102 percent in Georgia, and so on) has changed this. There are now more than 1 million Mexican immigrants in Alabama, Georgia, Tennessee and the Carolinas. Even Nashville, where one in thirteen residents is Latino, has a new *sonido*: the *norteño* music booming from its three Spanish-language radio stations. Los Tigres del Norte compete with Garth Brooks and *chipotle* compliments chitterlings across a vast stretch of the South, in urban "Little Mexicos" (like Nashville's Nolensville Road district) and mono-industrial company towns (like Houma, Louisiana or Dalton, Georgia) alike.[13]

Table 1
The Latino Core

Top Latino States (1997)		Top Latino Counties* (1997)		Top Latino Cities (1992)	
1. California	9,941,014	Los Angeles	4,000,642	New York	1,783,511
2. Texas	5,722,535	Dade (Fla.)	1,139,004	Los Angeles	1,391,411
3. New York	2,570,382	Cook (Ill.)	867,520	Chicago	545,852
4. Florida	2,105,689	Harris (Tex.)	852,177	San Antonio	520,282
5. Illinois	1,182,964	Orange (Cal.)	761,228	Houston	450,483

*New York City's five boroughs are treated by the Census Bureau as separate counties.
Source: Census estimates for 1992 and 1997 (September 1998).

Perhaps the most spectacular example of a sudden addiction to salsa is Las Vegas, the nation's fastest growing metropolitan area throughout the 1990s. Thirty years ago, the gambling oasis had hardly any Spanish-speaking residents, and the casino industry relied on a segregated Black population for its supply of maids and janitors. Today, nearly 200,000 Latinos outnumber Blacks in both "back-of-the-house" occupations and the general population. "Almost overnight, *taquerías,* money transfer outlets and immigration consultants have filled strip malls in new immigrant neighborhoods to the north and east of the strip. One roadside swap meet catering to immigrant Latinos in the adjacent city of North Las Vegas now draws an estimated 20,000 customers each weekend."[14] Some of this influx consists of families relocating from the deindustrialized neighborhoods of East Oakland and the dead copper towns of southern Arizona; but mostly it is spillover from the immigrant barrios of Los Angeles County. Extrapolations from current school-age demographics indicate that Latinos will become the majority in the city of Las Vegas within a decade.[15]

This far-reaching Latin Americanization of large and medium-sized central cities is being driven by a formidable demographic engine: a Spanish-surname population that is increasing by 1 million annually or (1990–96) ten times faster than the Anglo population.[16] While nativist hysteria has focused on supposedly "unrestricted" immigration, the growth of the Latino population is equally the consequence of higher fecundity in the context of larger families, especially amongst those of Mexican origin (two-thirds of all Latinos). The total fertility rate for women born in Mexico is more than double that of Anglo women.[17] Even if all immigration were ended tomorrow, the dramatically younger Latino population (median age twenty-six) would continue to increase rapidly at the statistical expense of aging, non-Hispanic whites (median age thirty-eight).[18] José, as a result, is now the most popular name for baby boys in both California and Texas, and Southern Californians are more likely to greet each other with "Qué tal?" than "Hey, dude."[19]

Table 2
The "Latinization" of the United States, 1950–2025
(Percent)

	Anglos	Blacks	Native Americans	Asians	Latinos
US Population					
1995	73.7	12.0	0.7	3.3	10.2
2025	62.4	13.0	0.8	6.2	17.6
California					
1995	52.6	6.9	0.6	10.7	20.6
2025	33.7	5.5	0.4	17.4	43.1
New York					
1995	66.6	14.5	0.3	4.5	14.0
2025	53.4	15.5	0.3	9.1	21.7
Texas					
1995	58.2	11.7	0.3	2.2	27.6
2025	46.0	12.8	0.3	3.4	37.6

Source: *Demographics Journal* and US Bureau of Economic Analysis.

More importantly, Spanish-surname children have since the late 1990s accounted for a larger share of the national school-age population than African-Americans, and Latinos are expected to displace Blacks as the largest minority before the end of the year 2000 – far ahead of earlier predictions.[20] Indeed if the 3.5 million US citizens in Puerto Rico are included as part of the national population, Latinos surpassed African-Americans at the beginning of the Clinton administration. Furthermore, the present demographic momentum will ensure that by 2025 there will be

16 million more Latinos (59 million) than Blacks (43 million). From then until mid-century, according to the Bureau of the Census, Latinos will supply fully two-thirds of US population growth. Shortly after 2050, non-Hispanic whites (25 percent of whom will be sixty-five or older) will become a minority group.[21] These are millennial transformations with truly millennial implications for US politics and culture.

Latinos, moreover, have a striking preference for big cities that contrasts with the crabgrass prejudices of an overwhelmingly suburban nation. (Only Asian-Americans are more urbanized.)[22] With the partial exception of Mexicans, who also invigorate small-town life from California (which had 72 Latino-majority cities in 1990) to Iowa,[23] all major Latino groups are heavily concentrated in the twenty largest cities, with Los Angeles and New York alone accounting for almost one-third of the national Spanish-surname population.[24] Having long boasted of being Mexico's second city, Los Angeles now also has a Salvadorean population equal to or greater than San Salvador.[25] New York City, meanwhile, has as many Puerto Ricans as San Juan and as many Dominicans as Santo Domingo. Without this Latino population boom, many big American cities would be dramatically shrinking in the face of accelerated white flight and, since 1990, Black out-migration. "The Greater Los Angeles and New York City metro areas," the *National Journal* notes, "each suffered a net loss of more than one million domestic migrants from 1990–95." Latinos, with help from Asian immigrants, compensated for this exodus to the edge cities and exurbs.[26]

The stubbornly binary discourse of American public culture

has, however, yet to register the historical significance of this ethnic transformation of the urban landscape. The living color of the contemporary big city, dynamically Asian as well as Latino, is still viewed on an old-fashioned black-and-white screen. (This is almost literally true: a recent study found that only one out of every fifty characters on primetime US television is a Latino.)[27] As Elizabeth Martínez notes, the 1992 Rodney King riots in Los Angeles County were universally interpreted as Black versus white or Black versus Korean, despite the fact that a majority of arrestees had Spanish surnames and came from immigrant neighborhoods severely battered by recession.[28] Similarly, when more than 75,000 young Latinos protesting anti-immigrant Proposition 187 marched out of their high schools throughout California in 1994 – the largest student protest in the state's history – it was virtually ignored by the media networks, although a comparable uprising by Black or white students would have become a national sensation.[29]

Unfortunately the invisibility of Latinos also extends to "high-end" urban studies. For more than a decade, urban theory has been intensely focused on trying to understand how the new world economy is reshaping the metropolis. Yet most of the literature on "globalization" has paradoxically ignored its most spectacular US expression. This neglect, moreover, is not for want of a richness of data and ideas. Researchers in the fields of Chicano, Puerto Rican and Cuban-American studies, as well as urban sociologists, anthropologists and immigration specialists, have produced a bumper crop of important findings and conceptual innovations that *soi disant* urban theory has failed to harvest.[30]

Moreover, Latino Studies recently has been capturing broad academic attention with its effective attacks on the great wall of US exceptionalism that has stood for so long between Latin American Studies and "American" Studies.[31] This little book explores some of the consequences of putting Latinos where they clearly belong: in the center of debate about the future of the American city.

2

BUSCANDO AMÉRICA

The Latino Metropolis is, in the first place, the crucible of far-reaching transformations in urban culture and ethnic identity. For half a century the designers of the US Census have struggled to create a category that would successfully capture all the individuals, regardless of race or household language, who share distinctive Latin American cultural roots. After early vacillations over whether Mexicans were a "race" (yes in 1930; no in 1940), several alternate statistical universes, including the category of "Persons of Spanish Mother Tongue" (1950) and "Spanish Surname" (1960), were tried and abandoned because of heavy numerical leakage. In population sampling for the 1990 Census, census workers simply asked people if they identified with any of twelve national identities: Mexican, Puerto Rican, Cuban and so on. Households with positive replies, independent of answers to other identity questions, were enumerated as "Hispanic" – a category adopted in the 1970s by the Nixon administration and first deployed in the 1980 Census.[32]

This is at best a bureaucratic expediency. In California and Texas, for example, "Latino" is generally preferred to "Hispanic," while in South Florida it is considered bad etiquette; on the East Coast both labels are common currency.[33] Scholars, meanwhile, have tried to draw battlelines between what they discern as different politics of usage. Juan Flores, for example, condemns "the superficiality and invidiousness of the term 'Hispanic' in its current bureaucratic usage." Agreeing with him, Suzanne Oboler (who devotes an entire book to the subject) and Rodolfo Acuña both claim that "Hispanic" is principally favored by eurocentric Spanish-surname elites in opposition to grassroots identification with "Latino." In the same vein, "to identify oneself today as a 'Hispanic,'" Neil Foley writes, "is partially to acknowledge one's ethnic heritage without surrendering one's 'whiteness.' Hispanic identity thus implies a kind of 'separate but equal' whiteness with a twist of salsa, enough to make one ethnically flavorful and culturally exotic without, however, compromising one's racial privilege as a White person."[34] Geoffrey Fox, on the other hand, argues that "'Hispanic,' with its emphasis on Spanish-language heritage as the foundation of meta-ethnicity, has no implied racial or class agendas and is simply preferred by most immigrants from Latin America."[35]

The debate is unlikely to be resolved. Indeed, there is broad critical awareness that both labels fail to acknowledge the decisive quotient of indigenous genetic and cultural heritage in the populations they describe. Both meta-categories, in fact, were originally nineteenth-century ideological impositions from Europe:

"Hispanicity" from Liberal Spain and "Latinity" from the France of Napoleon III.[36] Consanguinity (expunged, as Paul Edison has emphasized, of any indigenous component) was invoked to legitimize the reconquests attempted by both powers in the 1860s: France in Mexico and Spain in Santo Domingo.[37] Bolívar's and Martí's encompassing *Americanismo* meanwhile, has been stolen and parochialized by *los gringos*. It goes to the very heart of the history of the New World that there is no current, consensual term that adequately reflects the fusion of Iberian, African and "Indian" origins shared by so many tens of millions.

Moreover "Hispanic" and "Latino" can no longer be decoded as synonyms for "Catholic." Certainly syncretic New World Catholicism, with a thousand-and-one Aztec and African gods masquerading as *santos*, remains, together with the mother tongue, the most important common heritage of Latino immigrant communities. And few cross-cultural trends are as impressive as the recent flocking of other Latin American Catholics and even Anglo New-Agers to the cult of Mexico's Virgin of Guadalupe (who also reincarnates the powers of the goddess Tonantzin) as she has made her way *al otro lado*. (A digital laser replica of her image recently completed a triumphal procession of the Los Angeles archdiocese. "The 3-by-5-foot copy, blessed by the pope, toured some 50 local parishes before a farewell appearance in front of 50,000 worshippers at the L.A. Coliseum.")[38] Yet if murals of La Morena, radiant in her blue, star-studded shawl, sanctify the sides of *tiendas* from San Diego to Atlanta, the adjoining storefront will most likely be a Pentecostal church. Even in the city that the *pobladores* named "Nuestra Señora" (La Reina de Los Angeles),

Spanish-language Protestant denominations (especially Pente-
costals) are running neck-to-neck with the Pope. Latinos equally
reinvigorate US Catholicism (supplying 71 percent of its growth
since 1960) *and* energize its evangelical competitors.[39] In this new
dispensation, the traditional antinomy of Latino/Hispanic versus
Protestant collapses, and, as Carlos Monsiváis wryly suggests, the
immigrant may now pray to the Virgin of Guadalupe: *"Jefecita. I
am still faithful to you, who represents the Nation, even though I
now may be Pentecostal, Jehovah's Witness, Adventist, Baptist or
Mormon."*[40]

Table 3
US Latinos as a Latin American Nation
(Millions)

2000		2050	
1. Brazil	170.7	1. Brazil	241.0
2. Mexico	98.9	2. Mexico	144.9
3. Colombia	42.3	3. US Latinos	96.5
4. Argentina	37.0	4. Colombia	71.6
5. US Latinos	32.0	5. Argentina	54.5

Source: CEPAL (UN), "America Latina: Proyecciones de población, 1970–2050," *Boletín
Demográfico* 62 (July 1998). Other estimates put the US Latino population as high as 100
million by 2040.

Yet, if there is no reducible essence to *latinidad* – even in language or religion – it does not necessarily follow that there is no
substance. In playing with the Rubik's Cube of ethnicity, it is important to resist the temptation of prematurely resolving its con-
tradictions. "Hispanic/Latino" is not merely an artificial, racial-

ized box like "Asian-American," invented by the majority society to uncomfortably contain individuals of the most emphatically disparate national origins who may subsequently develop some loosely shared identity as a reaction-formation to this labeling. Nor is it simply a marketing ploy – like the right-wing Coors brewery's opportunist promotion of the 1980s as the "Decade of the Hispanic" – that exploits superficial national similarities in language, cuisine and fashion.[41] To be Latino in the United States is rather to participate in a unique process of cultural syncretism that may become a transformative template for the whole society. *Latinidad*, Flores emphasizes, has nothing to do with "post-modern aesthetic indeterminacy. ... It is *practice* rather than *representation* of Latino identity. And it is on this terrain that Latinos wage their cultural politics as a social movement."[42] As in Octavio Paz's famous definition of *mexicanidad*, to be Latino is "not an essence but a history."[43]

It is a history that will largely be made over the next generation. It has geopolitical significance because US Latinos are already the fifth largest "nation" in Latin America, and in a half-century they will be third only to Brazil and Mexico. Alternately, they will become the world's second largest Spanish-language-origin nation. Because contemporary US big cities contain the most diverse blendings of Latin American cultures in the entire hemisphere, they seem destined to play central roles in the reshaping of hemispheric as well as national US identities. There is a parallel here, of course, with the role of postwar London as a melting pot of anglophone Caribbean diasporas that has simultaneously transformed the meanings of "Englishness" and "Caribbeaness."

The dialectics of identity in the US case, however, are more complex because in each of the three cities that have made claims to be the "capital of Latin America" – Los Angeles, New York and Miami – the recipes for *latinidad* involve strikingly different national ingredients.

Table 4
National Composition of Latino Populations in the US, 1990

1. Los Angeles	Mexican (80%)	Salvadorean (6%)	Guatemalan (3%)
2. Miami	Cuban (66%)	Nicaraguan (11%)	Puerto Rican (6%)
3. New York	Puerto Rican (46%)	Dominican (15%)	Colombian (5%)
	Mexican (4%)	Ecuadorean (4%)	

Source: US Census 1990. What is hidden in these figures as well as ignored in most discussions of Latino identity is the rapidly growing population that identifies as multiple nationalities or heritages, ranging from, say, Mexican-Salvadorean to Cuban-Korean and Ecuadorean-Jewish. "Other" is the spanner in the works of the US ethnic-racial hierarchy.

Moreover, these national components themselves are not pregiven or unchanging essences. As immigration researchers have been reminding us since the days of Thomas and Znaniecki's monumental *The Polish Peasant in Europe and America* (1919), identities brought to the United States are reassembled into "ethnicities" within the contemporary force-field of the majority culture and its "others."[44] The complex and often conflicting elements of immigrants' previous identities, including fierce subnational allegiances to region and locality, as well as deep ideological divisions between religious and secular-radical subcultures, are strategically edited (and usually simplified) into usable ethnicities in the face of competing claims and pressures of other similarly constructed groups. Diasporic "Mexicanness" in El Paso, for example, does not mean the same thing as being Mexican *en la patria* just across the river in the twin city of Ciudad Juárez, just as being "Dominicanyork" or "Nuyorican" is significantly different from being Dominican in Santo Domingo or Boriquen in San Juan. (These, of course, are not necessarily exclusive identities, but situational identities between which individuals move back and forth in daily or annual itineraries.)[45]

Nor are ethnic identities necessarily stable over time. In Los Angeles, for example, each major generation of Mexican-origin youth has elaborated a different self-conception vis-à-vis Anglo society. Caught in a no-man's-land between ascriptive systems of race and ethnicity, "Mexican-Americans" in the 1930s through the 1950s expressed the pragmatic preference to be recognized as a hyphenated-ethnic minority along the lines of Polish- or Italian-Americans rather than to become a racialized caste like Blacks or Chinese.[46] Mexican-Americans during the 1940s and 1950s, Foley argues, signed a "Faustian pact with whiteness ... in order to overcome the worst features of Jim Crow segregation."[47]

Failed mobility and reinforced barrioization, together with the charismatic influence of militant Black nationalism, led "Chicanos" in the 1960s and 1970s to discard Mexican-American assimilationism in favor of separatist claims to an indigenous origin in a southwestern Aztlan.[48] (In privileging the myth of the Mexica, however, the Chicano movement unfortunately simplified a cultural heritage of magnificent diversity: Olmec, Tarascan, Zapotec, Mayan .... even Morisco and Converso.) The striking reemergence of *mexicanidad* in the 1980s and 1990s, on the other hand, is rooted in massive immigration and the expansion of the Spanish-language public sphere. (It is also, as we shall see later, an expression of the new structural synchronicity and intensification of ties between most immigrants' old and new homes.)[49] Recently, it has become popular in Southern California for young people to hyphenate their identities as either "Mexicana-Chicana" or "Chicana-Mexicana" depending on whether their families are first-generation immigrants or not.

Some Chicana/o intellectuals and writers, moreover, have tried to shift the debate about ethnicity beyond rhetorics of hyphenation. Like their counterparts in the "Irish Studies" movement, they are exploring the terrain that lies beyond the antinomies shaped by Anglo-Saxon colonization or the cultural reifications that ground traditional nationalism. Indeed, some of the most influential avantegardists, like Rubén Martínez and Guillermo Gómez-Peña, have embraced the "Border" – everything that represents the interpenetration of social formations and stands between simple choices of national identity – as a distinctively Latino and dialectical epistemology. ("We de-Mexicanized ourselves to Mexi-understand ourselves, some without wanting to, others on purpose. And one day, the border became our house, laboratory, and ministry of culture.")[50] Aptly titled *Frontera Magazine* – editorially committed to "poking around at the fringes, in the dustpiles and under the heaps of what's left over after all the definitions have been established" – provides a regular stage for the delirious subversion of reified ethnicity, as well as reaching that larger audience of young, hip Chicanos tuned into Culture Clash, Tijuana NO, and Rage Against the Machine.[51] Yet "post-nationalism" may have acquired its current purchase among border literati precisely because of the massive reassertion, over the last generation, of the physical and cultural continuity of Mexico in the US Southwest. Complex experiments in identity politics – unthinkable in the white-majority 1960s – are anchored in the confidence that Aztlan is no longer nationalist myth but historical fact.

For Puerto Ricans, by contrast, the national question is agonizingly unresolved and in some sense untranscendable, with a majority of the island's voters in a recent plebiscite endorsing "none of the above" rather than the Hobson's choice between culturally self-liquidating statehood and economically unviable independence.[52] The largest remaining nineteenth-century colony has by narrow but persistent electoral pluralities preferred the limbo of "commonwealth" to any definitive resolution of its status. As in the nearby French Antilles, *independistas* contribute decisive leadership to every social, labor and environmental struggle but, in the face of debilitating economic dependency, cannot find a fulcrum to enlarge their stable but tiny 5 percent of the vote.[53] This structural stalemate, together with the declining fortunes of the mainland diaspora (discussed in Chapter 10), gives Puerto Rican identity politics a traumatic urgency, sometimes bordering on revolutionary desperation (for example, the Macheteros), that is only reinforced by the US media's virtual blackout of island life. Indeed, as one *boriqueña* wryly suggests, the only thing visibly Puerto Rican in mainstream culture is Jennifer Lopez's voluptuous *culo*.[54]

Furthermore, these split-level processes of identity formation – the forging of ethnicity and meta-ethnicity – take place in regional contexts of unequal ethnic control over media and symbol systems. The programming of the 500 Spanish-language radio stations and two Spanish-language television networks in the United States often fails to reflect the true heterogeneity of Latino cultural and experiential worlds.[55] In Los Angeles, for example, Salvadoreans, Guatemalans and Ecuadoreans – as well as indigenous immigrants like Zapotecs, Yaquís, Kanjobals and Mixtecs – struggle to defend their distinctive identities within a hegemonically Mexican/Chicano popular culture.[56] In Chicago, on the other hand, comparably sized Mexican and Puerto Rican communities gingerly explore their cultural and political common ground, using *latinismo,* as Felix Padilla has shown, to leverage their clout within Cook County machine politics. (He usefully contrasts two modes of constructing *latinidad*: the fundamentally "weak" mode of passive, symbolic identification with a common language community; and the "strong" mode of active mobilization as an ethnic political bloc.)[57]

In Miami's Little Havana, meanwhile, the poorer Nicaraguan community (estimated Dade County population: 200,000) chafes under the cultural and economic dominance of Cuban elites. (With 5 percent of the national Latino population, Miami has nearly half of all Spanish-surname businesses.)[58] Although the Cuban percentage of Dade County's Spanish-surname population fell from 83 percent in 1970 to 66 percent in 1990, the counterrevolutionary agenda of aging exile leaders still exercises authoritarian censorship over Miami's major Latino cultural and media institutions, as well as influencing national Spanish-language television programming, which is skewed toward "white" Cuban-

American talk shows and Venezuelan *telenovelas*.[59] There has been considerable local resentment, sometimes expressed in public protest, against Miami's "exploitation" of the huge captive Spanish-language media markets in Los Angeles and New York.

Table 5
Largest Latino Markets, 1996

Market	Annual Retail Sales
1. Los Angeles	$28.9 billion
2. New York	$17.6 billion
3. Miami	$ 9.0 billion
4. San Francisco	$ 6.0 billion
5. Chicago	$ 6.0 billion

Source: Website: www.hispanic.market (1999).

In New York, by contrast, the Puerto Rican community, which in 1960 comprised four-fifths of the Latino population, now accounts less than two-fifths in the wake of the great Dominican migration of the 1980s and the new Mexican influx of the 1990s. (The Dominican population is now projected to surpass the Puerto Rican by 2010.)[60] The disappearance of a single dominant group has spurred intercultural exchange as well as competition between all the Spanish-speaking and Caribbean-origin communities. Latinization, moreover, has been intertwined warp and woof with New York's Caribbeanization. The racial diversity of New York Latinos, including so many black Puerto Ricans, Cubans and Dominicans, promotes, as Flores points out, a "more reciprocal and fluid relationship" to African-American culture.[61]

Younger writers and artists in *La Gran Manzana*, like the stellar Dominicanyorker Junot Diaz (*Drown*), openly advocate a radical politics of color. And, again in contrast to Los Angeles (where only 14 percent of married people of Mexican origin were married to someone from another ethnicity)[62] or Miami, fully half of the Spanish-surname marriages in New York are intermarriages between different Latino nationalities.[63] The cosmopolitan result is a rich, constantly evolving *sabor tropical* in food, music, fashion and language – always freshly spiced by the latest arrivals from Latin America.

Some prominent Latino intellectuals, embracing a messianic neo-Bolívarism, see in this New York–style cultural syncretism the seeds of new creolized identities on national, even hemispheric scales. "Ironically," writes Silvio Torres-Saillant, "Simon Bolívar's desideratum of a unified Latin American nation and the ideal upheld by Eugenio María de Hostos of an Antillean federation find in us a strange kind of fulfillment. We have come to articulate a collective identity, not in our native homelands, as Bolívar and Hostos had dreamed, but within the insecure space of the diaspora."[64] Likewise for Flores, Latinos are the new American counter-culture. "As each group and regional culture manifest itself in the new setting, and as they increasingly coalesce and interact in everyday life, New York is visibly becoming the source of a forceful, variegated alternative to mainstream North American culture."[65] Ilan Stavans, on the other hand, believes that the mainstream culture itself is being inexorably Latinized within a complex dialectic of transcultural exchange between old and new Americas. The rise of "Latinos *agringados*" addicted to hamburgers and Friday night football, he asserts, is tendentially balanced by the emergence of "gringos *hispanizados*" infatuated with chiles and merengue.[66] (He was writing before the current "cross-over" celebrity-boom of Selena, Ricky Martin, Christina Aguilera, Sammy Sosa and Jennifer Lopez.)[67] Similarly, the Brazilian futurist Alfredo Valladao, fascinated by the store signs in Miami and Los Angeles that say "Se habla inglés," sees the new Spanish-language "beachheads" in US cities as research laboratories for the cross-fertilization of North and South American cultures. The result, he confidently predicts, will be a new hegemonic global culture: "a Pan-American twenty-first century."[68]

3

LA FRONTERA'S SIAMESE TWINS

The Mexican–US border may not be the epochal marriage of cultures that Valladao has in mind, but it is nonetheless a lusty bastard offspring of its two parents. Consider, for example, *La Mona*. Five stories tall and buck-naked, "The Doll" struts her stuff in the dusty Tijuana suburb of Colonia Aeropuerto. Distressingly – to the gringo eye at least – she looks like the Statue of Liberty stripped and teased for a *Playboy* centerfold. In reality, she is the home of Armando Muñoz García and his family. Muñoz is an urban imaginer somewhere on a delirious spectrum between Marcel Duchamp and Las Vegas casino entrepreneur Steve Wynn. "Give me enough rebar and an oxyacetlylene torch," he boasts, "and I'll line the border with giant nude Amazons." In the meantime, he eats in *La Mona*'s belly and curls up to sleep inside her enormous breasts. When asked why he built a house with pubic hair and nipples, he growls back, "Why not?"

¿Porqué no? is an appropriate slogan for the West Coast's most

astounding metropolis. Like Swift's floating sky-city of Laputa in *Gulliver's Travels*, Tijuana seems to defy the ordinary laws of gravity. With an estimated 1.3 million inhabitants (1999), it is now larger than its rich twin, San Diego, as well as San Francisco, Portland and Seattle. Yet its formal economy and public budget are barely sufficient for a city one-third its size. Tijuana's urban infrastructure has always lagged at least a generation behind current demand. Grassroots audacity, symbolized by *La Mona*, makes up the difference.[69] Tijuaneses are consummate *bricoleurs* who have built a culturally vibrant metropolis from the bottom up, largely using recycled materials from the other side of the border.

A dusty rancho in 1900 and a gilded gambling spa for the Los Angeles movie colony during the 1920s, Tijuana became a boomtown during the Vietnam War expansion of the mid-1960s when urban Southern California began to import Mexican labor on a larger scale. Apart from some smaller Mexican border cities, the only city in North America to duplicate its explosive growth – and their population curves are uncannily synchronized – has been Las Vegas. The comparison is richly ironic since Mexican president Lázaro Cárdenas, rather than Bugsy Segal, has claim to be the true father of the glitterdome: it was his 1938 closure of Tijuana's Agua Caliente casino that sent the big gamblers and their Hollywood friends packing to Nevada.[70] Today, each of these instant cities unconsciously vies with the other in the replication of phantasmagoric urbanism.

The Border, however, easily trumps the Strip as surrealist landscape. Spanish offers the useful distinction between *La Línea*, the physical and jurisprudential border with its 230 million individual crossings each year, and *La Frontera*, the distinctive, 2000-mile-long zone of daily cultural and economic interchange it defines, with an estimated 8 million inhabitants.[71] All borders, of course, are historically specific institutions, and *La Línea*, even in its present Berlin Wall–like configuration, has never been intended to stop labor from migrating *al otro lado*. On the contrary, it functions like a dam, creating a reservoir of labor-power on the Mexican side of the border that can be tapped on demand via the secret aqueduct managed by *polleros, iguanas* and *coyotes* (as smugglers of workers and goods are locally known) for the farms of south Texas, the hotels of Las Vegas and the sweatshops of Los Angeles. At the same time, the Border Patrol maintains a dramatic show of force along the border to reassure voters that the threat of alien invasion (a phantom largely created by border militarization itself) is being contained. "The paradox of US–Mexico integration is that a barricaded border and a borderless economy are being constructed simultaneously."[72]

Although the escalation of border policing, as Peter Andreas shows in a brilliant study, only seems to promote the growth of more sophisticated and thoroughly criminalized smuggling, its failure as a practical deterrent generates "perverse consequences that increase pressures for more policing." "Perceptual impact and symbolic appeal" are the Border Patrol's real business: "In other words, this is ... a story about the political success of failing policies."[73] An increasingly Orwellian but deliberately porous border is the result. "This bizarre combination of ineffectuality and force at the border," writes Josiah Heyman, "determines the niches that undocumented immigrants occupy. In the border

area, immigrant peoples are both boundary-defined foreigners
and tacit, though bottom of the class structure, insiders."[74] In the
past, and still to a surprising extent today, the absence or nonen-
forcement of employer sanctions has ensured that only the workers themselves pay the cost of their "illegality" (in deportation,
lost wages, even imprisonment) – a powerful tool for intimidating
workers and discouraging unionization.

Table 6
Hypergrowth: Tijuana and Las Vegas

Year	Tijuana	Las Vegas
1950	65,000	48,283
1960	166,000	127,016
1970	341,000	273,288
1980	462,000	461,816
1990	747,000	784,682
1996	est 1.2 million	est 1.1 million
2000	est 1.3 million	est 1.3 million

Source: *Borderlink 1994*, San Diego State University 1994 (economic profile of the San
Diego–Tijuana region); Eugene Moehring, *Resort City in the Sun Belt: Las Vegas, 1930–1970*,
Reno, Nev. 1989; and Las Vegas Convention and Visitors Authority (1990 and 1996
figures).

The emergence of a dynamic *maquiladora* (*maquila* for short)
economy employing 1 million workers, 60 percent of them
women, in partial assembly operations on the border itself has
done little to stem the flow of surplus labor northward, since
Mexico adds 1 million more new workers each year than it can
actually employ in its formal economy. Indeed, the counterpoint
to the explosive growth of the border *maquila* economy has been
the drastic decline of Mexico's interior, home-market manufac-

turing.[75] In 1970, for example, Mexico had a larger and more advanced consumer electronics industry than either Taiwan or South Korea. But whereas competing Japanese and US multinational investment led to a dramatic increase in technology transfer and local sourcing in both Asian countries, US-owned electronics *maquilas,* Nichola Lowe and Martin Kenney have pointed out, "simply took advantage of Mexico's lower labor costs. As a result, these initial investments did not provide firms in Mexico's interior with the opportunity for establishing joint ventures or purchasing arrangements." Instead of incorporating indigenous firms into production alliances, the *maquilas* simply drove them into rapid extinction, a situation that has only worsened with the replacement of the US dinosaurs by the highly efficient Japanese *maquilas* with the captive supply chains.[76]

If border industrialization then sustains only a mirage of national economic development, it nonetheless has dramatically reshaped the culture of La Frontera and the inter-relationships of the dozen or so twin cities that span the border from Matamoros/Brownsville on the Gulf to Tijuana/San Diego on the Pacific.[77] The two largest and most dynamic of these binational metropolises are El Paso/Ciudad Juárez (1.5 million residents and 372 *maquilas*) and San Diego/Tijuana (4.3 million residents and 719 *maquilas*).[78] Despite some obvious differences, like the more radical abruptness of the socio-economic divide between San Diego and Tijuana, these pairs of *ciudades hermanas* are evolving along similar pathways that have few analogues within any other system of international frontiers.[79]

In both cases, *maquila* industrialization – led by garment and electronics assembly in Ciudad Juárez and television manufacture in "Tivijuana" (as locals call it) – has elaborated complex cross-border divisions of labor within larger webs of international trade. Within the framework of the North American Free Trade Agreement (NAFTA), adopted in 1994, Asian capital has played nearly as prominent a role as US investment in modernizing La Frontera. *Mexico Business Monthly* estimated in 1997 that *maquilas* source about 60 percent of their components from Asia versus 38 percent from the United States and just 2 percent from Mexico itself.[80] Nearly 40,000 Tijuanenses meanwhile work for Japanese *keiretsu* or Korean *chaebol,* many of which – like Sanyo and Samsung – have extensive distribution and engineering facilities across the fence in San Diego.[81] Although NAFTA is supposed to increase the North American content of maquila output dramatically, the US–Mexico border will likely remain Latin America's most dynamic interface with East Asia.

As La Frontera has become a major spoke in the Pacific Rim, old antinomies of development have given way to new paradoxes of integration. Whereas twenty years ago the most striking aspect of the border was the startling juxtaposition of opposites (Third World meets First World), today there is increasing interpenetration, in an almost magical-realist mode, of national temporalities, settlement forms and ecologies. Just as rows of ultramodern assembly plants now line the south side of the border, so have scrap wood and tar paper shantytowns become an increasingly common sight on the US side of the border. This urban-genetic exchange has only strengthened the distinctiveness of La Frontera as a transnational cultural system in its own right.

In Tijuana, Samsung, Sony, Sanyo and Hyundai dominate the *maquila* economy, master-planned industrial parks and postmodern company towns like Ciudad Industrial Nueva and El Florido – little kingdoms of "unlimited managerial prerogatives" or what Devon Peña calls "hyper-Toyotism" – directly abutt the border on the Mexican side.[82] *Maquila* managers commute to Tijuana's industrial zone every morning from lush San Diego suburbs like Chula Vista, while green-card-carrying Tijuanenses (officially known as "transmigrants") make the opposite commute by the thousands to work in San Diego's post-industrial tourist economy. Despite the enduring income precipice between the two sides of the border, social indicators no longer always point in one direction. While more than 40 percent of Tijuana's residents, for example, lack sewer hookups and running water, they can be proud that 90 percent of their school-age population actually attends school, in contrast to only 84 percent in far wealthier San Diego.[83]

In El Paso, on the other hand, more than 150 Mexican-style residential *colonias* (population 73,000), with minimal water supply or infrastructure, sprawl along the northern bank of the Rio Grande. Here persistent poverty on the US side of the border is equalizing residential landscapes to Third World conditions. "Drinking water," the magazine *BorderLines* explains, "is hauled in or acquired via shallow, dug wells that quickly become tainted by human waste, pesticide runoff, or heavy metals present in the surrounding soil. The water is kept in open, unsanitary containers – recepticles formerly used in industrial plants are a common method of storage, many still bearing labels that read 'not to be used for water.' One group of researchers recently discovered a

family using old ten-liter pesticide bottles to store water. Scarcity
means that water for bathing and cleaning comes from irrigation
ditches. Bathroom and kitchen wastes are usually disposed of in
septic tanks or open cesspools. Most *colonias* have no regular trash
collection. Given this situation, the grim health statistics of *colonias* are unsurprising." Due to the acute shortage of low-income
housing in border counties, 1.5 million poor US residents, Latinos
and a few Native Americans, are estimated to be living in shanty
colonias, principally in New Mexico and Texas.[84]

Maquila industrialization and runaway urbanization have also
spawned such terrible environmental problems that the National
Toxics Campaign now talks about the border as "a 2000-mile-long
Love Canal." The Tijuana River, for example, has until recently
discharged 12 million gallons of raw sewage daily on the San
Diego side of the border, while the New River, which flushes
Mexicali's sewage into California's Imperial Valley, has been described by the US Environmental Protection Agency as carrying
"almost every know viral and bacterial microorganism fatal to
human beings in the Western Hemisphere."[85] Conversely, US
firms are estimated to ship thirty times more hazardous waste
southward than Mexican firms send northward, despite NAFTA
regulations that outlaw environmental dumping and require toxic
by-products of assembly processes to be recycled in the country
originating the component or raw material.[86] Long a refuge for
US manufacturers fleeing environmental regulation, the Border
risks becoming North America's toxic sink. The danger is aggravated by the fiscal free ride offered to *maquila* capitalists, who pay
little or nothing in taxes for supporting infrastructure. Every

Mexican border city is forced to practice a triage of shifting scarce civic resources from poor neighborhoods to industrial parks: for example, clean water for the *maquilas* but none for the *colonias*. When workers or residents protest such conditions, as Heather Williams points out, they are the victims of punctual repression, facing dismissal, arrest, beating, even *desaparición*.[87]

Some macro-environmental problems, however, cannot be rendered invisible by state violence and, because they impinge directly on corporate profits or US quality of life, have necessitated novel binational initiatives. The siting of so many thirsty *maquilas* along the arid border, for example, has transformed a chronic water shortage on the Mexican side into a genuine emergency: one Samsung plant alone in Tijuana slurps up 5 percent of the city's annual water supply.[88] Because they share these indivisible ecological problems, the border's Siamese twins are slowly being compelled to integrate and transnationalize their urban infrastructures. In 1998 Mexican and US officials opened up the $440 million International Wastewater Treatment Plant which treats Tijuana's excess sewage on the San Diego side of the border, the first facility of its kind in the world. By 2010, San Diego and Tijuana water agencies are hoping to have constructed a binational aqueduct to the Colorado River. Similarly, El Paso and Ciudad Juárez – blanketed with the same smog – are currently discussing the creation of a unified air quality district.[89]

In each case, moreover, binational approaches to local environmental management (and, potentially, to law enforcement) are strengthening the "New Federalism" in Mexico along lines passionately advocated by the neoliberal opposition party, the PAN, which currently governs several key border states.[90] This weakening of ites to the national center in tandem with the proliferation of so many new cross-border alliances and collaborations is a profound disturbance in the national equilibrium of Mexican politics. Some nationalist writers have compared it to the unsettling influx of US capital and influence into northern Mexico in the years just before the Revolution. Yankee xenophobes, sleepless over the threatened "take-over" of the Southwest, have their anxious counterparts in the D.F. (Districto Federal), biting their fingernails over the potential secession of El Norte.

The ultimate configuration of national and transnational loyalties will depend on how both sides of the border deal with the new physical hazards and social problems created by President Clinton's unilateral militarization of the border in 1994. In the NAFTA era, capital, like pollution, may flow freely across the border, but labor migration faces unprecedented criminalization and repression. In an attempt to steal the wedge issue of "uncontrolled immigration" from the Republicans, Clinton (cheered on by California senators Diane Feinstein and Barbara Boxer) massed Border Patrol personnel on the San Diego/Tijuana border ("Operation Gatekeeper") and prodded Congress to double the armed agent force of the Patrol and its parent, the Immigration and Naturalization Agency.[91] With help from the Pentagon, surveillance of key border sectors has been automated with seismic sensors that pick up the tiny "earthquakes" of immigrants' footsteps. Other futuristic border-control gimmicks, including "an electronic current that stops a fleeing car, a camera that can see into vehicles for hidden passengers, and a computer that checks commuters by voiceprint," are being studied at San Diego's Border Research and Technology Center, which was established in 1995 specifically to support Operation Gatekeeper with cutting-edge military and CIA technologies.[92]

At the same time, the principal battleground of the "War on Drugs" has been shifted from Colombia and the Andean countries to the Mexican border, where the US military, including elite Marine reconnaissance units, provides covert backup to the Drug Enforcement Administration and the Border Patrol. As Andreas notes, "The logics of US drug and immigration control are in many ways similar: the foreign supply is defined as the primary source of the problem and deterring the supply through enhanced policing is promoted as the optimal solution."[93] In practice, the distinctions between immigration control and narcotics interdiction, or between policing and low-intensity warfare, have become so blurred that border-dwellers speak routinely of the "war against drugs *and* immigrants."[94]

It is a war, moreover, with many real casualties. In recent years the highly publicized crackdowns on twin-city borders (nearly 1 million arrests per year) have forced more immigrants to attempt dangerous crossings on remote stretches of the Rio Grande or through furnace-hot southwestern deserts. By one estimate, nearly 1,600 have died as a result, including a group of ten who perished of thirst in the desert east of San Diego in August 1998.[95] Others have been killed in increasingly violent encounters with the Border Patrol, or, in the case of Esequiel Hernández, a teenager from the US border community of Redford, Texas in an ambush in 1997 by Marines looking for drug smugglers. Few Americans outside of La Frontera are aware of how entangled federal law enforcement agencies and the military have become in regulating the daily lives of border communities.[96] As one Laredo city councilmember complained after the shooting of Hernández, "I already feel like we are living under martial law here." Amnesty International agrees that "cruel, inhuman or degrading treatment," of US citizens as well as undocumented immigrants, has become disturbingly common, and in a 1999 visit to Tijuana, High Commissioner for Human Rights Mary Robinson (the former president of Ireland) expressed the United Nations' growing concern with the humanitarian crisis on the border.[97]

The popular perception of a transnational police state along the border has been reinforced by President Zedillo's sweeping deployment of the Mexican army in open contempt of the constitution to conduct arbitrary searches of civilians and mount highway checkpoints. Mexican law was also violated in 1998 when more than 100 elite "Special Forces" police were used to herd strikebreakers through picket lines at a Tijuana feeder plant for Hyundai Motors. The government's iron-fisted response to the first strike by a genuinely independent *maquiladora* union may prefigure a violent future for industrial relations along the border. In the neoliberal utopia of the border economy capitalized on Mexico's catastrophic national level of unemployment, real wages bear little or no relationship to workers' productivity or their cost of living. Despite "a tight labor market, high productivity, and record profits," the *maquilas* "have yielded successively lower wages for the people who work in them. In real dollar terms, the average wage rate in the *maquiladoras* has declined by a staggering 65 per cent since salary peaks in that sector in 1981."[98]

The government's efficiency in suppressing the seeds of labor militancy contrasts, of course, with its famous inability to arrest the notorious border drug barons, supposedly the most wanted men in the hemisphere, as they brazenly lounge at Caliente race-track or boogie the night away in trendy discos. The two warring cartels based in Ciudad Juárez and Tijuana now control much of North America's drug imports, intercepting the cash flow that formerly returned to Medellín and Calí. They effectively consti-tute the invisible third government of La Frontera. With Andean-sized drug profits has come Colombian-scale drug violence in-volving the comprehensive collusion of police and military officials. In 1994, Tijuana (which fifty years earlier had been Al Capone's favorite resort) became the arena of spectacular broad-daylight gunbattles between corrupted police forces allied with competing cartels. In a single two-month period, writes Sebastian Rotella, "The state police, in league with drug lords, were accused of killing a federal commander in a shoot-out. An assassin had killed the presidential candidate [Luis Donaldo Colosio], whose own campaign guards were suspects in the assassination. The fed-eral police, in league with drug lords, were suspected of killing the city police chief. The federal police had arrested the deputy state attorney general and charged him with corruption." By 1997 as many as 600 murders annually were being attributed by human rights activists to *narcotraficantes* or their bad cop henchmen.[99]

In September 1998 the drug war produced a slaughter of inno-cents. A dozen gunmen working for an affiliate of Tijuana's Arel-lano-Félix cartel forced twenty-one people from their beds in the

Ensenada suburb of El Sauzal, ordered them to lie face down on a concrete patio, and opened fire with automatic weapons. Nineteen of them were killed, including infants, small children and a pregnant woman. The victims were members of the Pai-Pai tribe, one of Baja California's few remaining pre-Columbian communities. After narrowly escaping extermination in the nineteenth century, the Pai-Pai hid out for decades in a mountain fastness of the Baja California desert before being "rediscovered" by Sierra Club hikers in the 1950s. The massacre apparently was the climax to a long struggle over the cartel's use of communal Indian lands for marijuana cultivation and clandestine airstrips.[100]

For more upscale carnage, including the assassinations of prosecutors, police chiefs and newspaper editors, the Arellano-Félix syndicate prefers to recruit its gunmen, not from local *colonias*, but from the meaner streets of San Diego's slums. This is the *Clockwork Orange* version of binational urbanism. It was Arellano mercenaries from San Diego's Thirtieth Street gang, armed with automatic weapons, who gunned down Cardinal Posadas Ocampo of Guadalajara in 1993 and then carried out a sensational string of drive-by killings in luxurious San Diego suburbs. The sinister image of an armor-plated Chevy Suburban (many of its parts manufactured in *maquiladoras*) spewing deadly AK-47 fire out of its windows has become a popular icon of the transnational gangsterism celebrated in Border rap as well as traditional *corridos*. Unsolved murders (including those of 171 young female *maquiladora* workers in Ciudad Juárez since 1993) are just part of the day's freight in the brave new world being created by NAFTA.[101]

4

THE LATINO METROPOLIS

The distinctiveness of La Frontera as a social formation has not gone unrecognized. "Border Studies" itself has become a transnational industry centered on Mexico's unique El Colegio de la Frontera Norte (founded in 1984), with offices in virtually every border town and research partners in big California, Arizona and Texas universities.[102] Surprisingly little attention, on the other hand, has been focused on the historical geography of Latino settlement patterns in nonborder cities, although in at least one case (metropolitan Los Angeles) the reality is unparalleled.[103] As emergent Latino pluralities and majorities outgrow the classic barrio, they are remaking urban space in novel ways that cannot be assimilated to the earlier experiences of either African-Americans or European immigrants. Moreover, while urban sociologists and historians use familiar categories like the "second ghetto" to encompass the common evolution of Black communities on a national scale, the major Latino metropolises are strikingly different in their spatial economies. As a provisional typology, the predominantly Latino areas of US big cities can be classified according to their spatial complexity (rather than mere size).

Table 7
Typology of Latino Urban Areas

1. Primate barrio with small satellites	Los Angeles 1960
2. Polycentric barrios	Chicago 1990
3. Multicultural mosaic	New York 1990
4. City-within-a-city	Los Angeles 1990

In the classic Chicago School model of the North American city, the ethnic district is a simple wedge – Deutschland, Russian Town, Little Sicily, Black Belt and so on – driven into the concentric circles represented by different housing/income classes. Mexican settlement in Los Angeles before 1970 closely approximated this idealtype with a single primate barrio east of the Los Angeles River that contained the majority of the Spanish-surname population. This is a pattern that still applies to cities like Oakland, Philadelphia, Phoenix, Houston, Atlanta and Washington, D.C.

A second, more complex residential geography is represented by contemporary Chicago, where a majority of the Spanish-speaking population is concentrated in four, roughly equal-sized districts. Although Back of the Yards on the southwest side and South Chicago were the original ports of entry for Mexican railroad and stockyard workers in the 1920s, the capital of the Mexican diaspora in the Midwest today is Pilsen and the adjoining neighborhood of Little Village (its original Czech residents called it Cesca California). Benito Juarez High School, the Rudy Lozano Public Library, the Mexican Fine Arts Museum and Calle Mexico testify to the vibrant community – life built by five generations of working-class immigrants from Mexico's Bajío region. Puerto Rican Chicago over the decades has moved from West Town to contiguous Humboldt Park and Logan Square (the 31st Ward). Serious riots broke out in the barrio in 1966 and again in 1977 after the killing of local youngsters by police.[104]

Gotham, of course, is an extraordinary quiltwork (see Figure 1). The 880-page atlas of New York's Latino population published by the Institute for Puerto Rican Policy in 1996 identified no less than twenty-one major Latino neighborhoods in four boroughs, including eleven predominantly Puerto Rican areas in the south half of the Bronx, two majority Dominican neighborhoods in upper Manhattan (Washington Heights and Morningside Heights), and two mixed South American enclaves in Queens. In contrast to Los Angeles, which has many barrios and smaller, incorporated cities with Spanish-surname populations in excess of 90 percent, all of New York's Latino neighborhoods have large non-Latino minorities (African-American, Asian, Black Caribbean, new European, etc.) of 30 to 45 percent. Even on a fairly micro level, New York is far more pluricultural than any other major metropolitan core.[105]

All three spatial types – primate district, polycentric neighborhoods, ethnic mosaic – recapitulate previous American urban ecologies. Los Angeles, however, is a case apart. The map in Fig-

Figure 1 Spanish Surnames in New York, 1990

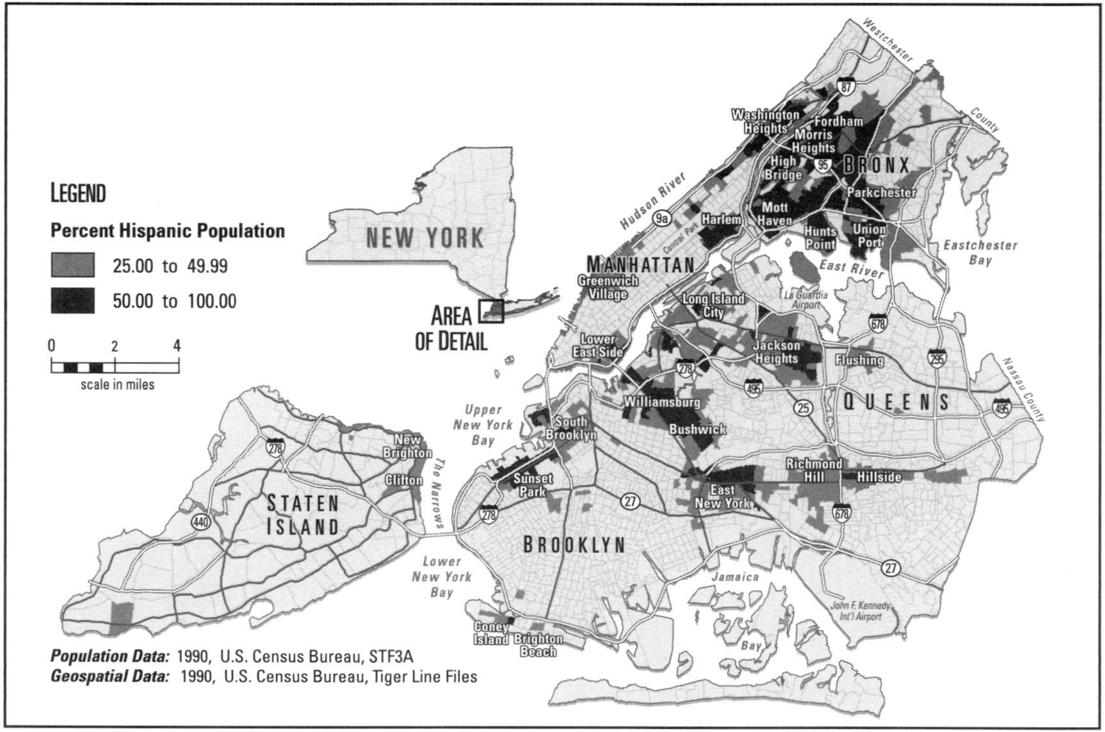

LEGEND

Percent Hispanic Population

25.00 to 49.99

50.00 to 100.00

0   2   4
scale in miles

Population Data: 1990, U.S. Census Bureau, STF3A
Geospatial Data: 1990, U.S. Census Bureau, Tiger Line Files

ure 2 depicts a geography without obvious precedent. In trying to
decipher its spatial structure, I have compared its "footprint" to
those of other major ethnic or linguistic minorities in bicultural
cities: Kleindeutschland in 1870s New York (when German speak-
ers were 30 percent of the population),[106] Blacks in 1960s Chicago, Anglophones on the west side of Montreal, Anglos in San
Antonio and so on. In every instance, the second language or
racial group is concentrated in one or two sprawling districts with
various small outliers. There is none of the complex fractal ge-
ometry that characterizes Latino Los Angeles with its hundred
Spanish-speaking neighborhoods and subdivisions radiating from
the old Eastside core. Indeed the Latino population is now so
large – currently more than 5 million in the Los Angeles-Orange
County SMSA – that perceptual figure-foreground reversal is im-
minent. The Anglo-majority neighborhoods, mostly near the
beach or in the foothills, are becoming a gilded periphery to the
bustling Latino metropolis in the coastal plain, whose 21st-cen-
tury outline (all the 25 percent to 49 percent Spanish-surname
1990 census tracts will likely have Latino majorities in the 2000
census) is clearly legible.

The spatial logic of this vast city-within-a-city, so mysterious
on first examination, is easily revealed by overlaying a map of
industrial land-use zoning. Latinos occupy almost all of Los Angeles and Orange County's traditional blue-collar housing tracts
and suburbs adjacent to the three great corridors of industrially
zoned land along Interstate 5, the 60 (Pomona) Freeway, and the
Los Angeles River. Latino L.A.'s gravitational center is the old
Central Manufacturing District: the vast sprawl of aging facto-

ries, warehouses and classification yards immediately southeast
of Downtown. This geography has been generated in a single
generation by the "browning" of Los Angeles's industrial working class. Residential succession recapitulates economic restructuring as Latinos have become predominant in low-tech manufacturing, home construction, and tourist-leisure services. During
the last quarter-century, Latinos have replaced blue-collar Anglos
(who have moved inland in large numbers to western San Bernardino and Riverside Counties) in the quadrant of industrial suburbs southeast of Downtown, as well as in the northeast San
Fernando Valley, the western San Gabriel Valley and northern
Orange County. (Orange County, the holy land of Nixon-Reagan
Republicanism, is rapidly polarizing between blue-collar, majority
Latino north county and professional-managerial, overwhelmingly white south county.) Mexican and Salvadorean immigrants
likewise have superceded working-class African-Americans on the
east side of Southcentral Los Angeles. (Central Avenue, the old
main street of Black Los Angeles, is now 75 percent Latino.)[107]

In Los Angeles's new ethnic division of labor, Anglos tend to
be concentrated in private-sector management and entertainment
production, Asians in professions and light industry, African-
Americans in civil service occupations, and Latinos in labor-inten-
sive services and manufacture. New York, by contrast, retains a
more multi-ethnic working class than Los Angeles, while Miami
has a more significant Spanish-surname capitalist class. Latino
ethnic succession in Los Angeles is taking place primarily at the
base of the post-Fordist occupational pyramid. Although tens of
thousands of Spanish-surname businesses testify to a huge pool

Figure 2 Spanish Surnames in Los Angeles, 1990

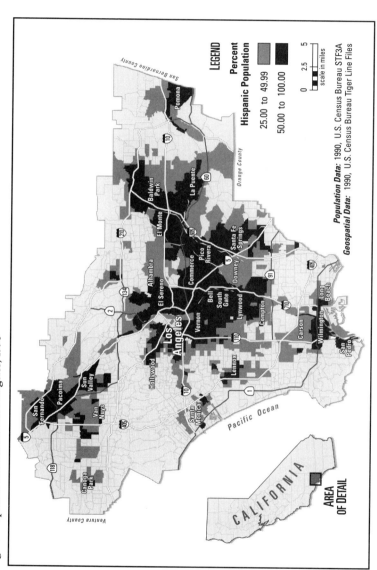

of entrepreneurial energy, the capitalization of Latino enterprises is generally minuscule and the largest locally owned firm remains a tortilla company. Apart from the Televisa / Univision media empire, there has been surprisingly little flow of corporate investment from Mexico into Los Angeles's giant Spanish-language consumer markets. Although tens of billions of dollars of expatriated Mexican capital has been floating around Southern California since the financial perturbations of the late 1980s, most of it is apparently salted away in *Fortune* 500 stocks or beachfront real estate.

Asian capital, by contrast, has eagerly sought out Latinos as both workers and consumers. Los Angeles County has its own enclaved import / export platform economy, the counterpart to a *maquiladora* zone, located in the eponymous industrial suburbs of Commerce, Industry and Vernon. Here, 75,000 to 100,000 Latino immigrants are directly employed by diasporic Chinese manufacturers and wholesalers in plants often "twinned" with sister facilities in Taipei, Guangzhou or Tijuana. Likewise, Korean investors control thousands of low-income residential units in inner-city neighborhoods as well as the larger share of the "swap meet" space that dominates retail trade in Southcentral Los Angeles. New Asian and Latino residents, in addition, rub shoulders in Hollywood and a dozen other neighborhoods west of Downtown, while upwardly mobile Chicanos and affluent Chinese immigrants live side-by-side in the dim-sum-*con-salsa* suburbs of the eastern San Gabriel Valley. Indeed, Los Angeles is distinguished from other metropolitan areas by the extraordinary scale and economic importance of the daily interactions between its Asian and

Figure 3 L.A. Population Living Below the Poverty Level, 1990

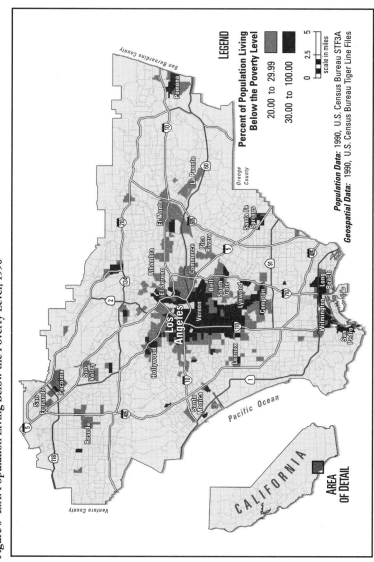

LEGEND

**Percent of Population Living
Below the Poverty Level**

20.00 to 29.99

30.00 to 100.00

scale in miles

0   2.5   5

Population Data: 1990, U.S. Census Bureau STF3A

Geospatial Data: 1990, U.S. Census Bureau Tiger Line Files

San Bernardino County

Pomona

La Puente

El Monte

Santa Fe Springs

Orange County

Alhambra

Pico Rivera

Commerce

El Sereno

Bell

South Gate

Lynwood

Compton

Vernon

Los Angeles

Hollywood

Lennox

Long Beach

Wilmington

San Pedro

San Valley

Pacoima

San Fernando

Reseda

Santa Monica

Pacific Ocean

Ventura County

CALIFORNIA

AREA
OF DETAIL

Latino immigrants. Thus it is not entirely surprising that Spanish rather than English is the obligatory second language of many immigrant Asian entrepreneurs.[108]

Within this Latino metropolis there are clearly legible spatial and socio-economic distinctions between new immigrants (Mexican and Central American) and second- to fifth-generation Chicanos.[109] According to the 1990 Census, the Mexican-origin population was almost equally split between the Mexican-born and the US-born, with half of the Mexican-born arriving in a huge devaluation-driven wave after 1980. The superimposition of a map of 20 percent or higher poverty over a base map of Spanish-surname census tracts thus vividly distinguishes between a poor, new-immigrant core, clustered around Downtown and Southcentral Los Angeles, and a more affluent Chicano suburban belt (containing a majority of the 400,000 Latino households earning more than $35,000 annually) in the San Gabriel Valley. The same dualistic mapping emerges if Spanish-language usage or voter registration is substituted for household poverty. In the central districts, Spanish is the idiom of daily life in 80 percent or more of households, while in the majority Chicano suburbs it is the primary language in less than 40 percent of homes. Similarly, the predominantly immigrant neighborhoods have exceedingly low percentages of enfranchised adults compared to the vote-rich San Gabriel Valley – the most important Latino political constituency in the nation. However, it should be recalled that these are variegations in a cultural continuum and that other factors – especially immigrants' arrival cohort (say, between those who came before and those who came after 1980) – are usually more decisive in shaping

opportunity structures than whether residents identify most
strongly as Mexicanos or Chicanos. What is most striking in any
comparative perspective is the cultural unity and blue-collar solid-
ity of Mexican Los Angeles. The Anglo conquest of California in
the late 1840s has proven to be a very transient fact indeed.

5

TROPICALIZING COLD URBAN SPACE

Latinos are bringing redemptive energies to the neglected, worn-out cores and inner suburbs of many metropolitan areas. The process is most vivid in cities, especially in the Southwest, where immigrants have access to homeownership, even if that involves the leveraging of mortgages through the combination of three or even four low-wage adult incomes. A remarkable case is the belt of old (circa 1920) bungalow neighborhoods directly south and southeast of Downtown Los Angeles. Here, in the aftermath of the 1965 Watts riot, bank "redlining," civic indifference and absentee landlordism accelerated the decay of an aging, poorly built housing stock. Yet today, even in the historically poorest census tracts, including most of the Central-Vernon, Florence-Firestone and Watts-Willowbrook districts, there is not a street that has not been dramatically brightened by new immigrants. Tired, sad little homes undergo miraculous re-vivifications: their peeling facades repainted, sagging roofs and porches rebuilt, and yellowing lawns replanted in cacti and azaleas. Cumulatively the sweat equity of 75,000 or so Mexican and Salvadorean homeowners has become an unexcelled constructive force (the opposite of white flight) working to restore debilitated neighborhoods to trim respectability. Moreover, the insatiable immigrant demand for family housing has allowed older African- American residents to reap unexpected gains in home sales: a serendipitous aspect of "ethnic succession" that has been ignored by analysts who focus only on the rough edges of Black/Latino relations.[110]

Immigrant homeowners are indeed anonymous heroes. No medals have been handed out for community reinvestment nor has the City of Los Angeles – which has thrown away hundreds of millions in tax dollars unsuccessfully trying to induce middle-class professionals to gentrify downtown – ever geared its redevelopment programs to support, rather than displace, inner-city homeowners. Instead Latino immigrants (and here Los Angeles rejoins the general case) are confronted with a labyrinth of laws, regulations and prejudices that frustrate, even criminalize, their attempts to build vibrant neighborhoods. Their worst enemies include conventional zoning and building codes (abetted by mortgage lending practices) that afford every loophole to developers who airdrop over-sized, "instant-slum" apartment complexes into formerly single-family neighborhoods, but prevent homeowners themselves from adding legal additions to accommodate relatives or renters. Although medium-density infill, with rental income accruing to resident homeowners, is obviously a better solution, even ecologically, for housing the rising low-income populations in Southwestern cities, it is hardly ever accommodated by law or building practice. As a result, there is a proliferation of boot-legged, substandard garage and basement conversions that keep Latino homeowners embroiled in costly conflicts with city building inspectors.

Likewise there is unending guerrilla warfare over commercial uses of residential and street space. Latino "micro-entrepreneurship" is applauded in theory but everywhere persecuted in practice. If the primordial zoning division between home and work is annoying for cybercommuters and self-employed professionals, it is truly punitive for Latino households whose incomes are supplemented by home-based car repair, food catering or bridal sewing. Many cities and suburbs have similarly restricted or even outlawed the weekend garage sales and informal street-curb "swap meets" that are such important institutions in barrio economies. The bitterest struggles, however, have arisen over street-vending and street-corner labor markets. Unlike Latin American or Caribbean cities, the North American metropolis preserves no traditional juridical or physical space for the survival economy of the poor (witness the shameful way that the homeless have been pushed to the wall). As a result, staggering law enforcement resources have been wasted in New York and Los Angeles in cruel harassment of the vendors who refresh streetcorners (often to the delight of gringo commuters) with their sale of *paletas, champurrado* and *tamales*. From Portland to Long Island, police are also often called to deal with the "problem" of *esquineros* clamouring for work in front of hardware and paint stores. Only grudgingly have city halls made truce with their hardest-working residents and adopted the commonsense solution of formally establishing street-vending precincts and day-labor parks equipped with sanitary facilities.

Inter-cultural skirmishes also take place on purely audio-visual fronts. Neighborhood aesthetic wars have become commonplace as Latino carnivality collides with the psychosexual anxieties of *Truman Show* white residential culture. Thus the glorious sorbet palette of Mexican and Caribbean house paint – *verde limón, rosa mexicano, azul añil, morado* – is perceived as sheer visual terrorism by non-Hispanic homeowners who believe that their equity directly depends upon a neighborhood color order of subdued pastels and white picket fences. Even upwardly mobile Chicanos have joined in the backlash against "un-American" hues, as in the L.A. suburb of South Gate where the City Council recently weighed an ordinance against tropical house colors, or in San Antonio where writer Sandra Cisneros has long outraged city fathers with her deeply expressive purple home. And the same Puritan spirit that once sent the police to quell all-night "hoolies" in Irish kitchens now calls 911 to complain about lively *quinceañeras* or *fiestas familiares*. In many communities, noise ordinances, like curfews, have become a form of racial profiling. (As a Chicano friend, who lives in an Orange County suburb, once complained: "Heavy metal is cool, but *banda* is a misdeamenor.")

In the most fundamental sense, the Latinos are struggling to reconfigure the "cold" frozen geometries of the old spatial order to accomodate a "hotter," more exuberant urbanism. Across the vast pan-American range of cultural nuance, the social reproduction of *latinidad*, however defined, presupposes a rich proliferation of public space. The most intense and creative convergence of Ibero-Mediterranean and Meso-American cultures is precisely their shared conviction that civilized sociality is constituted in the daily intercourse of the *plaza* and *mercado*. (Historians of Borbon Mexico, for example, have had traditional difficulty disentangling the elements of colonial town planning that are Spanish in origin from those that are indigenous.) Latin American immigrants and their children, perhaps more than any other element in the population, exult in playgrounds, parks, squares, libraries and other endangered species of US public space, and thus form one of the most important constituencies for the preservation of our urban commons.

They also have a genius for transforming dead urban spaces into convivial social places. Who (except for Mayor Giuliani) is not heartened by the rebirth of La Colonia's derelict lots as tropical gardens and outdoor restaurants? What monolith of corporate sculpture brooding over a fountain in a bank plaza can compete with the great community murals of EastLos, the Mission District or Pilsen? Thirty years ago, Pacific Avenue in L.A.'s blue-collar suburb of Huntington Park was another geriatric Main Street with little future beyond the Salvation Army outlet. Today it reigns in restored art-deco glory as the shopping and festive center of Mexican immigrant life in Los Angeles County: the focal point for the thousands of revelers who spontaneously gather every time *la patria* wins a championship or World Cup playoff. Likewise, hip Chicano art dealers and booksellers have given sleepy downtown Whittier – Dick Nixon's hometown – a new lease on life, making it, in effect, the west San Gabriel Valley's Greenwich Village. Other Latino bohemias are sprouting in

San Jose, Tucson, Denver, San Antonio, Austin and, of course, New York.

Yet again mainstream planning and architectural theory lag far behind grassroots urban imagination. Almost a generation ago, Los Angeles's pioneer Chicano urban design firm, Barrio Planners, boldly proposed to retrofit Eastside neighborhoods with small plazas, each of which would become a colorful stage for local identity. "Let a hundred *placitas* bloom!" was the slogan, but the concept of reshaping urban space to celebrate Mexican culture or, even more radically, to stimulate neighborhood self-design, was not well received by a planning bureaucracy still committed – consciously or unconsciously – to architectural Americanization. Los Angeles city and county planners instead allowed private speculators to build almost 2000 minimalls in the late 1970s and early 1980s (most of them, ironically, in Taco-Bell moderne). Neighborhoods were drowned in junk retail space guarded by armies of minimum-wage security guards whose principal duty is to reduce "loitering" and other nonprofit activities. In the meantime, the barrios are still starved for lack of parks or usable open space. The one populist proposal to win reluctant city hall approval – a tiny "mariachi plaza" in Boyle Heights – has taken more than twenty years to come to fruition.

As Barrio Planners long ago foresaw, the emergent "Latino metropolis" requires its own design strategy, a counter-plan not merely to resist the dumping of noxious land uses (the toxic industries, landfills, jails and freeways that despoil Latino communities across the country) but to elaborate its own audacious cultural hegemony. The seeds for visionary activism, of course, are already planted. All of Latin America is now a dynamo turning the lights back on in the dead spaces of North American cities. While there is much abstract talk in planning and architectural schools about the need to "reurbanize" American cities, there is little recognition that Latino and Asian immigrants are already doing so on an epic scale. Perhaps the time is ripe (as Latinos locally move from minority to majority politics) to tropicalize the national vision of "the city on the hill."

6

THE THIRD BORDER

The first step in any Latino urban agenda must be to remove *La Migra* from the front yard. Visitors to Southern California are often shocked by the huge INS checkpoints – a veritable second border – that blockade the major Interstate freeways at San Clemente and Temecula, fifty to sixty miles north of Tijuana. Intended to intercept *coyotes* smuggling immigrants into Los Angeles and to reassure white suburbanites that Washington really is "in control," the controversial checkpoints have become for most Latinos hated symbols of an INS police state with sweeping powers far away from the border. They are blatant instances of racial profiling as federal policy. Even the Chicano assistant district attorney, whose grandfather fought as a Marine at Guadalcanal, will tense a little and experience anew an ancient humiliation as he inches his shiny Lexus past the scrutiny of the Border Patrol in their sinister dark glasses. (Perhaps thinking to himself: "Goddamn Irish-Americans don't have to go through this.")[111]

For those genuinely *sin papeles,* the checkpoints, especially at San Clemente (a stone's throw from Nixon's former "Western White House"), are often deathtraps. To avoid discovery, smugglers unload their cargo a mile or two before the checkpoint and order them to cross to the other side of the freeway and make their way along the beach (part of the vast Camp Pendleton Marine base) until they are safely north of the INS. Crossing ten lanes of high-speed Interstate freeway, congested until the early morning with heavy truck and tourist traffic, is a desperate gamble for anyone, but for tired and disoriented immigrants, many of whom have never seen a freeway before, it is often suicidal. Over the last fifteen years, more than a hundred people have been killed, including whole families mowed down while running hand-in-hand: at one point, there was a therapy group in San Diego for traumatized drivers who had accidentally hit freeway crossers. After spending a million dollars studying every option, except closing the San Clemente checkpoint, California's state transportation agency, Caltrans, created the world's first official "pedestrian accident zone" in the late 1980s, replete with bizarre warning signs that depict a frightened family bolting across the highway. It was a moral threshold in the naturalization of the daily violence of immigration.

But the border doesn't end at San Clemente. Indeed, as any ten-year-old in East L.A., or Philly's el Norte knows, borders tend to follow working-class Latinos wherever they live and regardless of how long they have been in the United States. In suburban Los Angeles and Chicago, for instance, the interface between affluent

Anglo majorities and growing blue-collar Latino populations is regulated by what can only be typed a "third border." Whereas the second border nominally reinforces the international border, the third border polices daily intercourse between two citizen communities: its outrageousness is redoubled by the hypocrisy and cant used to justify its existence. Invisible to most Anglos, it slaps Latinos across the face.

Consider the San Gabriel Valley, just east of the City of Los Angeles. Once the center of the California citrus industry, the Valley, with nearly 2 million residents, is a mature, built-out suburban landscape politically fragmented into more than forty separate shards, ranging from large secondary cities like Pasadena and Pomona to unincorporated country "islands" and special-use incorporations like City of Industry and Irwindale. Although the great orchards were subdivided into tract homes a half-century ago, the fundamental division inherited from the citrus era between a Chicano/Mexican working class and an Anglo gentry continues to frame all social relations in the Valley. The traditional demographic balance, however, has been overturned, with roughly three Latino residents for every two Anglos by the early 1990s. Moreover, there is also a growing Chicano managerial-professional class, as well as a massive new Chinese immigration (approximately 250,000) that is all the more spectacular because it has taken the form of an eight-mile-long linear Chinatown extending eastward through Monterey Park, Alhambra and San Gabriel.

Although Anglo blue-collar residents have largely left the southern tier of Valley towns where they were formerly a majority, the wealthy foothill tier from La Cañada/Flintridge to Clare-mont remains highly attractive to young white professionals as well as to traditional elites. If the Valley floor has become the Chicano Democratic heartland, the foothill suburbs are still Rea-gan Republican and organized massively in support of anti-immi-grant Proposition 187 in 1996. Here, amidst the sharpest ethnic and class tensions, a third border has arisen most obnoxiously to restrict the use of public space by poorer Latinos from nearby communities.

One example is the boundary between El Sereno and South Pasadena. El Sereno is an outlier of the City of Los Angeles in the western San Gabriel Valley. It is a well-groomed but aging blue-collar suburb, home to hardworking truckdrivers, medical secre-taries and postal workers with last names like Hernandez and Rodriguez. South Pasadena, on the other hand, looks like Andy Hardy's hometown – big Midwestern-style family homes on quiet tree-lined streets – incongruously inserted into the Los Angeles urban fabric. Most importantly, its median home values are at least $100,000 higher than El Sereno's.

Some years ago when South Pasadena was still lilly white, the city fathers decided that the twain must never meet and engi-neered the barricading of busy Van Horne Street. It may not be the old Berlin Wall, but to those on its "bad side" it insultingly stigmatizes their neighhorhood as a violent slum. Serenos were especially incensed when South Pasadena justified the street clo-sure in the name of "preventing drive-by shootings." Since many older Chicanos tell bitter stories of harassment by the South Pasadena police, it is not surprising that they regard the barricade with the same fondness that Black southerners once felt about segregated drinking fountains.

San Marino, just to the east of South Pasadena, is one of the nation's wealthiest suburbs. It embalms ancient regional dynasties like the Chandlers of the *L.A. Times* and until recently provided a national headquarters for the John Birch Society. In recent years some of the Latino housecleaners and gardeners who keep its lush lifestyles scrubbed and pruned began to bring their own families on weekends to San Marino's beautiful Lacy Park. But the appearance of "aliens" – nannies pushing their own kids in prams not their mistresses' – in their cherished park incited near-hysteria, and the City Council obliged residents by imposing a weekend, nonresident use-fee of $12 per family – unprecedented in Los Angeles County. (Incredibly, the council justified the fee by claiming that the city was nearly broke.) Similarly, San Marino's crown jewel, the world-renowned Huntington Library and Gardens (built on the surplus value created by Henry Huntington's Mexican track laborers) changed its traditional free admission ("donation requested") to a strictly enforced $8 per head: another deterrent to diversity amidst the roses.

Arcadia, home of the famous Santa Anita racetrack (and Proposition 187's "godfather," State Senator Richard Mountjoy), has an even worse reputation among Valley Latinos. Historically it was one of the few citrus-belt towns that refused to allow its Mexican workers to live anywhere within the city limits, even on the other side of the tracks. In 1939, while Hitler was promulgating anti-Semitic laws, 99 percent of Arcadia's burghers signed a unique public "covenant," promoted by a local escrow company,

that promised to keep their piece of paradise "Caucasian forever."
They have never stopped trying. Thus when Arcadia's sprawling
Wilderness Park became popular with Spanish-speaking families
in the early 1990s, there was an even uglier uproar than in San
Marino. "I've seen their graffiti," ranted a leader of the neighbor-
ing Highland Oaks Homeowner's Association. "I've heard their
ghettoblasters ... I don't want any riffraff coming into our city."
The mayor agreed: "The park has been overrun with *these* people." As a result, Arcadia restricted public use of the park, now
officially a "wilderness center," to a single eight-hour period on
Fridays.

So far there has been little legal challenge to the foothill communities' legislation of exclusionary barriers, but in suburban
Chicago, where Latinos are now the largest minority in 112 out of
149 incorporated communities, the Justice Department has had
to file suit to prevent what critics have termed "city-sponsored
ethnic cleansing." Thus in western suburban Addison, following a
large Latino influx in the 1980s, the village purchased and destroyed most of a sprawling apartment complex that was the center of an immigrant community. In charging Addison with violat-
ing the Fair Housing Act, an assistant attorney general observed,
"This is not urban renewal, it is urban destruction motivated by
the national origin of the residents."[112] Similarly, the Illinois Attorney General's Office denounced inner-suburban Cicero
(whose Latino population exploded from 8.6 percent in 1980 to 37
percent in 1990) for using illegal occupancy ordinances to stop
Latinization. "The town has made no secret that it wanted to limit
the number of Hispanics." (The state pressed the same case

against occupancy laws intended to limited the population of "La Selva" [the Jungle], an area of nearby Franklin Park.)[113]

Northwest suburban Rosemont, on the other hand, has taken the extraordinary step of publically financing the walling-off of the affluent half of its population from poorer Latino residents. "Unlike the town's two apartment and condo neighborhoods, Scott Street has 24-hour, police-manned checkpoints and video cameras that record license plates – all paid for by the village. Although Rosemont is nearly 20 per cent Latino, the Scott subdivision is 95 per cent white." Supporters of the Rosemont *laager* point out that they have simply extended the regionally ubiquitous cul-de-sac (metropolitan Chicago has thousands of Van Horne Street–type barricades or cul-de-sacs demarcating racial and socio-economic borders) to its logical conclusion. Originally designed to wall-in Black residential areas, cul-de-sacs are now the first line of defense against Latino ethnic succession in Chicago's aging, inner suburbs.[114] Roberto Suro's reassurance that Anglos nationally accept Latino immigrants "as an unobtrusive [and necessary] appendage to their new suburban culture" obviously applies only to the earliest stages of the relationship.[115]

7

FABRICATING THE
"BROWN PERIL"

Flashback: The banquet room of a popular restaurant in Santa Ana, California. It is fall 1994, a few weeks before the passage of Proposition 187, which proposes to expel the children of undocumented immigrants from schools and deny prenatal care to their mothers. For two years Republican Governor Pete Wilson has been stoking white anger about the "invasion of California" and the sleaze talk-show belt on AM radio is dominated by shrill denunciations of new immigrants and their children. The martyred icon of white anxiety is a San Clemente high school student, Steven Woods, who was supposedly murdered in 1993 by Mexican gangbangers in a local beach parking lot. "Los Amigos," a service network for Orange County Latino professionals, has just finished a breakfast discussion of the Woods case and its exploitation by the Prop. 187 campaign. The families of several of Woods's accused assailants are present. I listen to their version of events.[116]

Elena Penuelas's nightmare is always the same. First there is the gruesome image of the dead boy. His eyes are wide open but empty. A steel rod protrudes from one side of his head. Then follow the helpless figures of her own sons, Hector and Saul, who are manacled and mute in their orange jail jumpsuits. Guards drag them down a long, dark corridor. They disappear forever. Suddenly people are screaming at Elena in English, a language she does not understand. As the angry din increases, the noise turns to water. It engulfs everything. The world begins to dissolve. "Nos estamos ahogando," she says through her tears. "We are drowning."

Seated across the table, María Bonilla Vásquez solemnly nods her head. "Sí, ahogando." She knows that Elena's nightmare is painfully real. Her own teenage son Julio, together with Hector Penuelas, has just been convicted of second-degree murder. Altogether, five out of six young Mexican men charged in the case will receive 17- to 25-year murder sentences for the death of Steven Woods, although none of them is specifically accused of the actual act. The case is a dark mirror of class and ethnic hatred in the wealthy, conservative suburbs of southern Orange County.

The Penuelases and the Pérez Bonillas, like many of their neighbors, come from a poor *ejido* near the town of Silao in the Mexican state of Guanajuato. (There are an estimated 2 million Guanajuatenses in the United States; 800,000 live in Houston and Dallas, and a majority of the rest are in Metropolitan Los Angeles and Chicago.)[117] They migrated together – a village of farmers and artisans transformed into a small mobile army of gardeners, janitors and housekeepers – to San Clemente, the "Spanish Village by the Sea" founded by Seattle's strikebreaking former mayor Ole Hanson in the early 1920s. Most Americans remember it as the home of Dick Nixon's "Western White House."

Elena Penuelas, who works as a maid, recalled her first view of the famous red-tiled roofs of *faux*-Spanish San Clemente: "It looked like paradise ... the most beautiful place any of us had ever seen." In the beginning, at least, the Anglos seemed to welcome the quiet, diligent immigrants who cleaned their pools, changed their babies' diapers and blow-dried their lawns. But at San Clemente High School, where haughty *Beverly Hills 90210* wannabes resented the influx of poor Latinos, there was growing tension. The kids from Silao, many of whom could barely speak English, bore the brunt of racial slurs and crude "beaner" jokes. Some, like eighteen-year-old Saul Penuelas, found the daily humiliation intolerable and dropped out to work full-time. His younger brother Hector, sixteen, buried himself in the extracurricular fervor of Youth for Christ. Others, like their friend Julio, stayed in school but gravitated to the protective periphery of the VCs (Varrio Chico), the town's traditional Chicano gang.

On the evening of 15 October 1993, following a Friday night football game, San Clemente High's two worlds inadvertently confronted each other in the parking lot of Califia Beach Country Park. Seventeen-year-old Steven Woods and four carloads of friends were partying at the bottom of the lot, while a dozen Mexican kids, including Pérez Bonilla and the Penuelas brothers, were parked at the top. Both groups had been drinking beer. The Anglo teenagers later admitted that they drove their cars "very fast," with headlights off, toward the exit where the Mexican youngsters were standing. Woods's friends claimed they were merely trying to escape after one of their group had been slapped by Julio Pérez Bonilla, who was mad because the boy had flipped him the finger earlier in the week.

Hector Penuelas, on the other hand, testified that four vehicles, led by an ominous black Chevy Suburban with tinted side windows, "were coming directly at us, and we were scared. We thought they were trying to run us over." In fright and anger, Hector threw a block of wood and Julio, a short length of copper pipe. Neither of the missiles inflicted damage. Meanwhile, the rest of the group hurled beer cans, an old badminton racket and several paint rollers – all debris from the back of the Penuelases's pickup (their dad is a housepainter).

The clash lasted but a few seconds and involved only the first two cars. Although some of the Mexican kids heard a window break, they had no inkling that anyone had been injured. (Steven Woods was not visible behind the lead vehicle's tinted windows.) Their sole intention had been to stand their ground, to show courage. Perhaps on Monday there would be more respect at school *para la raza*. In the meantime, they all went home to get ready for their weekend jobs – unaware that they were about to become Orange County's most infamous "street terrorists." They did not know that one of the paint rollers, spinning end over end, boomerang-like, without its carriage – had broken the passenger-side window of the first car and pierced Woods's brain. Defenders of the San Clemente Six would later point out "the astronomical odds against a paint roller hitting any predetermined point associated with a rapidly accelerating car." Even the investigating sher-

iff conceded that it was a "fluke," and officials of the Orange
County Crime Lab complained that it took them hours of experimentation before they were able to puncture drywall with an
identical roller.

Steven Woods vegetated in a coma for almost a month before
dying. His mother – a widow who had lost two other children –
lashed officials with her tearful demands for revenge. (She would
later file a lawsuit against the Mexican kids' parents, lead a recall
campaign against one of the judges in the case, and star in an
Emmy Award–winning documentary.) In the meantime, the
shared responsibility of both teenage groups for the tragedy at
Calafia Beach (as well as the ineffable quotient of sheer accident)
was transformed into a demonic allegory about a "wilding" pack
of immigrant gang predators and their "innocent victims." Although an aggressively driven vehicle might be considered a more
lethal weapon than a badminton racket or paint roller, authorities
automatically discounted the Mexican teenagers' version of
events. The local media meanwhile created the illusion that a
singularly cold-blooded, premeditated murder had been committed. Thus the *Orange County Register* – a paper so right-wing that it
has blamed minimum-wage legislation for gang violence – spread
the fiction that "a gang member [deliberately] rammed a metal
rod through Woods' head." The *Los Angeles Times,* for its part,
transformed Woods into "a symbol of tragic proportions" for
south Orange County residents fearing a sudden deluge of "violent, urban-style crime" in "their quiet coastal haven."

Of the nine Mexican youths arrested at their homes or workplaces early on 16 October, six were ultimately indicted. Horrified

by Woods's death, and assured by police that charges against his
friends would be dropped if he confessed, Arturo Villalobos admitted that he had thrown a paint roller, although he had no idea
whether or not it was the one that speared Woods. Elena Penuelas
confirms that Arturo was deliberately tricked. None of his friends
was released as promised: instead, while he was entering a guilty
plea to voluntary manslaughter, they were arraigned for murder.
They were eventually convicted in a set of trials which Los Amigos and other Latino groups denounced as "complete travesties."

Perhaps the most shocking trial involved Hector and Julio, who
were minors at the time of Woods's death but were tried as adults.
Although neither was accused of throwing the lethal roller, they
were quickly convicted, not only of second-degree murder, but of
eight accessory felony counts including assault, conspiracy and
"street terrorism" (gang membership). The court-appointed defense
attorneys inexplicably waived the right to a jury trial despite the pre-
siding judge's draconian reputation. Neither lawyer could understand Spanish nor directly communicate with the boys' families.
Both sets of parents complained bitterly that they were kept in the
dark about trial strategy. In his summation, the prosecutor characterized Youth for Christ activist Hector and conscientious student
Julio as "wild dogs." Under terrific political pressure to set an example against "gang terror" in Orange County, Judge Everett Dickey
discounted every atom of the defense case. "If the defendants feared
for their safety," he argued, "then all they had to do was get off the
roadway." More importantly, "since the motivation for the attack was
the same for all those involved," they were "equally responsible for
Steve Woods' death." QED.

Woods's mother meanwhile became an anguished presence at "Save Our State" (SOS) rallies in support of Proposition 187. The wording of the proposition declared that the people of California "have suffered and are suffering economic hardship caused by the presence of illegal aliens in this state [and] are suffering injury and damage caused by the criminal conduct of illegal aliens in this state." A macabre x-ray photograph of the paint rod in Steven Woods's brain was circulated as what-else-need-be-said? proof of this criminal conduct. San Clemente High School students staged a one-day walkout and hung a provocative banner, "Take Back Our City," over Interstate 5. Local pro-Prop. 187 newsletters spewed Himmlerian warnings about the "stench of urination, defecation, narcotics, savagery and death" associated with Latin and Asian immigration. Swastikas appeared on statues at Our Lady of Fatima Catholic Church in San Clemente, and the families of the San Clemente Six received numerous death threats. Because of their sons' notoriety, the Penuelases, all nine of them, were evicted by their landlord and forced to camp in a relative's living room.

Two weeks after the first convictions in the Woods case, moreover, the largest criminal taskforce in local history swept through the sprawling "superbarrio" – centered on Santa Ana but also straddling Anaheim, Fullerton, Orange and Garden Grove – that segregates two-thirds of Orange County's almost 800,000 Latino residents. With Governor Pete Wilson sharing the photo opportunity, District Attorney Michael Caprizzi announced the arrest of 123 members and associates of the "notoriously vicious" Sixth Street gang. Their names, all Spanish surnames except for two,

were prominently displayed in the *Register.* It was a million dollars' worth of free publicity for Proposition 187. In fact, the
imaginatively titled "Operation Roundup," with its confirming
images of Latino criminality, was largely a hoax. The Santa Ana
Police, something of a rogue power in a Latino-majority city still
governed by Anglos in 1994, had deliberately padded the body
count with children as young as twelve and some very low-level
misdemeanants. In trawling the streets near the Civic Center, for
example, they had arrested fugitives from such warrants as an
unpaid dog license, drinking in public, driving too slowly in traffic
and having improper mud guards.

As Los Amigos emphasized at the time, the case of the San
Clemente Six and the ensuing panic about Latino gangs bear an
uncanny resemblance to Los Angeles's notorious Sleepy Lagoon
incident of 1942. In what was then the largest murder trial in US
history, nine Eastside teenagers were sent to San Quentin for a
supposed gang killing, although none was identified as the actual
assailant and the forensic evidence was rubbish. Alice McGrath,
who was the executive secretary of the original Sleepy Lagoon
Defense Committee and the real-life model for Alice Bloomfield
in Luis Valdez's play *Zoot Suit,* has been an outspoken supporter
of the San Clemente defendants. "All the fundamental elements –
the grotesquely slanted press coverage, the assumption of collective guilt, the biased judge, and so on – remain the same," she told
me in 1994. "Just as the hysteria around Sleepy Lagoon (largely
stirred up by the *Los Angeles Times*) fed the bigotry that erupted in
the so-called Zoot Suit Riots of 1943, so the San Clemente case
became a lightning rod for today's nativists. The manipulation of

Mrs. Woods as a symbol of middle-class vengeance is particularly disturbing." She does however see a major difference between the two cases: "The general atmosphere was not so intolerant in the 1940s. Progressive sentiment was much stronger. Our committee drew support from a huge spectrum of Black, Jewish, left and labor movements. Orson Welles, Rita Hayworth and Anthony Quinn even came down from Hollywood to help. The current situation is much darker. These are the meanest times I have ever seen in California."

In Orange County and elsewhere, the new "brown peril" became the moral equivalent of the obsolete red menace. The leading historian of Latinos in Orange County, U.C. Irvine's Gilbert Gonzalez, contrasts the traditional stereotype of the "docile, dawn-to-dusk Mexican citrus laborer" with "Anglo kids' new socialization into an image of Latinos as a violent criminal class." Law enforcement groups have been among the most blatant ethnic stereotypers. The Santa Ana Police Officers Association enraged residents with an election mailer that juxtaposed portraits of Mexican toddlers holding rifles taller than themselves with photographs of armed teenage gangmembers. The caption: "When their baby pictures look like these, this is how they grow up." With such incitements to prejudice it is not surprising that some foes of immigration believed that they had been issued a hunting license ("187" is the California Penal Code number for murder).

In January 1995 a self-appointed vigilante, William Masters, II, shot two unarmed youths, whom he derided as "skinhead Mexicans," while they were painting graffiti on a Hollywood freeway overpass. Rene Arce, eighteen, died immediately, and David Hilo, twenty, was wounded. Neither of the young men had a criminal record. The *Los Angeles Times* reported that police "were overwhelmed by dozens of calls from graffiti-haters supporting Masters." Attorneys volunteered to represent him, while other residents offered money for a possible defense fund. One man showed up at the jail, saying that he wanted to take Masters to dinner for performing a "profound service to the community." Outraged Latino community leaders demanded Masters's indictment for manslaughter, but District Attorney Gil Garcetti let him go and arrested Hilo for vandalism instead. As Masters snarled after his release: "Where are you going to find twelve citizens to convict me?"[118]

8

TRANSNATIONAL SUBURBS

In 1982 a terrible fire raced through an aged tenement building near downtown Los Angeles, killing twenty-four women and children. Fire department investigators were astounded to discover that the several hundred residents of the structure were all neighbors from a single village, El Salitre, in the Mexican state of Zacatecas. Overwhelmed by debt, drought and devaluation, half of El Salitre had been sent *al norte* to help rebuild communal fortunes. Tragedy thus revealed a fundamental structural characteristic of the emergent Latino metropolis: the basic building blocks of Spanish-speaking urban neighborhoods are not only individuals and households, but entire transnationalized communities. To earn their living and reproduce their traditional solidarities, hundreds of *ejidos, rancherías,* villages and small towns in Mexico, Central America and the Caribbean have had to learn how to live like quantum particles in two places at once.

It is important to distinguish between old and new patterns of

chain migration. Since the days of Ellis Island, it has been common for advance guards of male immigrants to build employment niches in particular communities or workplaces to which
they recruited *paisanos* from their home clan, village or region.
These niches and networks over time became invaluable "social
capital" for the sending communities, enabling them to export
unemployment, acquire new skills, leverage their financial resources, and insure themselves against vagaries of nature and the
world market. In the past they were maintained by young men
(or, more rarely, young women) who worked for periods ranging
from a few seasons to a decade or more in the United States, then
returned, often in honor and with renewed fortune, to their native communities. A significant minority, of course, stayed on the
other side of the border or ocean and eventually brought their
families over to join them. But the basic pattern, equally characteristic of Mexicans in the 1970s as Italians in the 1900s, was the
temporary or seasonal flux of manpower adjusted to the rising or
falling labor-market demand in the metropolis.

During the *década perdida* of the 1980s, as debt crisis grew into
depression for millions of Mexicans and savage US-sponsored
civil wars engulfed Central America, the "push" factors in emigration became more inexorable. Poverty in Mexico, for example,
soared from 28.5 percent of the population in 1984 to 36 percent
in 1996.[119] "Between 1982 and 1991," writes UNAM economist
Julio Moguel, "salaries paid to laborers in manufacturing industries lost 36% of their purchasing power. The real wages of white-
collar workers in those same industries fell 22%, and the value of
social services fell 23%. But the hardest hit lived in the country-

side. Average real wages paid to agricultural workers fell 51% over that same period. At the same time, the gap between rich and poor was colossal. In 1990, just over 2% of the Mexican population received 78.55% of the national income."[120]

Regardless of economic conditions (the "pull" factors) in the United States or the dangers posed by a more militarized border, the sheer survival needs of households and communities have dictated the increasingly difficult and dangerous trek northward. ("Vamos al norte a luchar por la vida," the young were commanded.) Immigrant flows previously absorbed by Mexico City were redirected toward Southern California and New York. Young women began to join the northward exodus in significant numbers, as did unemployed skilled workers and declassé urban professionals. Meanwhile, the 1986 reform of US immigration law created both carrot (amnesty for 3.1 million previously illegal immigrants) and stick (employer sanctions and militarization of the border) to encourage cyclical labor migrants to seek permanent residency. Established immigrants with work permits increasingly used their legal advantage to reunite their families in the United States. They also began to make unprecedented investments in US homes, college educations and small businesses.[121] Some observers have mistakenly interpreted this increased commitment to US domicile as a sign of diminished identification with traditional homes and cultures.

Immigrants have, in fact, had to entrench themselves more securely on the northern side of the border in order to defend their embattled social identity in the south. ("Mexico," writes Carlos Monsiváis, "has evolved from a sedentary country to a nomadic one."[122]) More than ever, repatriated "migradollars" (an estimated $8 billion to $10 billion annually during the 1990s) are a principal resource for rural communities throughout Mexico and Central America. Surpassing sugar and coffee, they are now the largest source of foreign exchange in the Dominican and Salvadorean economies.[123] As a result of the increasing "incorporation of migration cultures into the very adaptive fabric of the [local] social system," entire communities have become effectively transnationalized.[124] The new logic of social reproduction under conditions of rapid and sometimes catastrophic global restructuring compels traditional communities to strategically balance assets and population between two different, place-rooted existences. Economic and cultural umbilical cords now permanently connect hundreds of Latin American and Caribbean localities with counterpart urban neighborhoods in the United States. To the extent that the sending communities have become as fully integrated into the economy of the immigrant metropolis as their own nation-state (a process that some researchers call *Nortenización*),[125] they are the de facto "transnational suburbs" of New York, Los Angeles, Chicago and Miami. Indeed, they transform our understanding of the contemporary big city.

It is important to emphasize that this is not merely metaphor, but involves radical new social and geographical lifelines that have been forged by the cunning of communities and households adjudged most "expendable" by the invisible hand of the planetary marketplace. Pueblos whose genius for adaptive mutation allowed them to endure, first the Conquest, then the Porfiriato, now find that cultural survival in an age of cyber-capital requires strategic mitosis, dividing themselves into two parts to sustain a single heredity. In his study of how the rural *municipio* of Aguililla in southwest Michoacán has cloned itself in the Silicon Valley suburb of Redwood City, Roger Rouse argues that "Aguilillans have become skilled exponents of a cultural bifocality that defies reduction to a singular order ... Today it is the [transmigration] circuit as a whole rather than any one locale that constitutes the principal setting in which Aguilillans orchestrate their lives."[126] Similarly, Hetcher writes of the residents of another Michoacán community, Napízaro, that has transplanted itself to the San Fernando Valley: "Unable to secure a full livelihood either in Mexico or in the United States, migrants must extend their families and their households across the border, thus creating transnational households and a transnational conlmunity."[127]

US employers, in turn, have become skilled at exploiting the "positive externalities" like free labor recruitment and superb workgroup discipline that arise from organized communal emigration. Robert Suro cites the extraordinary case of Randall's, a high-end Houston grocery chain that has recruited more than 1000 workers (all Evangelicals) from closely related villages in the Totonicapan highlands of Guatemala. "Out amid the freeways and strip malls," Suro found a thriving Mayan village improbably housed in "a cluster of faux Georgian low-rise apartment houses."[128] The link to Randall's and Houston has become so vital in Totonicapan that it has been incorporated into local religious ritual:

Every July for many years, the Maya have celebrated a weeklong festival in the narrow streets of San Cristobal. And every year, dozens, sometimes hundreds, of the Houston expatriates have made a point of coming home on vacation at that time of the year. These return trips have become ritualized, a part of the fiesta itself, and the migration north is commemorated along with the harvests, old saints, and timely weather. On the last day of the fiesta, the entire town gathers to watch a soccer game between a team of Houston Maya and the hometown all-stars. And each year when the festivities end, the channel between Texas and Totonicapan has become busier and more efficient.[129]

Ironically, these communal survival strategies have been powerfully assisted by the very technologies that are commonly identified with globalism and delocalization. Looking at how the villagers of Ticuani, now equally split between Puebla and Brooklyn, maintain their powerful sense of corporate identity, Robert Smith points to the revolutionary roles of telecommunications and cheap airfares. "The point is that instantaneous communications and rapid travel make it possible for today's immigrants and their second-generation children simultaneously to maintain significant lives or at least to have significant lived experience in their communities of origin and destination. This in turn enables some social forms 'imported' from the old country to persist and be adapted to the new one, and for Ticuanenses in New York to influence life there."[130]

The Ticuanenses have reconstituted themselves into a "virtual village," where all important communal business is debated in weekly conference calls between elders in Brooklyn and Mexico. Ties with the old home are regularly renewed by family vacations and frequent participation in village festivals, while intense team volleyball rivalries with other immigrant associations provide a passionate focus for Ticuanense identity in Brooklyn. (The Oaxaqueño diaspora uses basketball tournaments for the same purpose.)[131] At the same time, the diasporans loyally maintain the all-important flow of migradollars back home. Since the 1970s, the Ticuani Solidarity Committee in New York City has financed an extensive modernization of the pueblo, building two new schools and renovating the church and municipal buildings. Within this intense network of communal activity, with its manifold real-time links to Mexico, the closed corporate structures of the village world – including *compadrazgo* (godparentship) and the political-religious hierarchy of the *cargo* (self-government) system – thrive in face of the otherwise corrosive influence of US urban culture. As Smith points out, while previous generations of immigrants from Ireland or Italy may have had similar goals, "The fact that they could not go home for the weekend or negotiate with their counterparts in the village via speaker phone as do the Ticuanenses today, makes the quality and quantity of relations on the micro level quite different."[132]

Immigrants from the depressed state of Zacatecas use a beauty contest – the annual competition for the crown of Señorita Zacatecas – as social cement to organize their diaspora. With half of its 2 million population north of the border (principally in Los Angeles County), Zacatecas has become the Mexican state most completely dependent upon the export of its labor. (In Los Angeles, the fiestas of the forty-nine hometown clubs that comprise the Federación de Clubes Zacatecanos recall the huge Iowa Day picnics of the 1930s.) In recognition of this, the state's political machinery is becoming binationalized. "Both Zacatecas gubernatorial candidates campaigned in California last year [1998], despite the fact that US residents could not vote. One of the first official acts of the victor, Ricardo Monreal Avila, was to appoint a representative in Los Angeles, the core of the expatriate community, and he has asked the Zacatecas state legislature to create two additional seats for US residents – a first for Mexico."[133]

Although American diasporas have always played prominent roles in the political life of their homelands through fundraising and lobbying US foreign policy (think of Irish Republicanism or Zionism), they can now participate directly and simultaneously in national political life. The huge Dominican community in Manhattan and Queens is another spectacular case in point. During the authoritarian presidency of Joaquín Balaguer, imposed by a US invasion in 1965, leading Dominican dissidents were shunted off to exile in New York, which became the main base for the country's oppositional politics. Even after the relaxation of political repression in Santo Domingo, New York has remained the second home for the republic's turbulent political life.[134] Indeed, the Dominican Republic is the first country in Latin America and the Caribbean to elect a transnational migrant as president. As the New York Times marveled last year, "The Dominican President Leonel Fernandez Reyna grew up on the Upper West Side, still holds a green card, and has said he intends to rejoin his family in Manhattan at the end of his term."[135] Both the Dominican and Mexican congresses are currently considering legislation that would allow immigrants to vote in the United States: the final step in full electoral transnationalization. (The 10 million adults currently possessing or eligible for Mexican citizenship in the United States would comprise 15 percent of the country's electorate, or a bigger voting bloc than Mexico City.)[136]

Alternatively, some immigrants have brought their political systems with them. In Los Angeles, for example, thousands of Zapotec immigrants from Oaxaca, as well as transporting their local saints and madonnas northward, have also transplanted their traditional village governments *en bloc* to specific inner-city Catholic parishes. These councils have earned a formidable reputation for their skill in negotiating the quotidian difficulties of immigrant existence:

> The Zapotecs outmaneuver slumlords by buying apartment buildings – which the church dutifully blesses – listing multiple names on the titles and paying for them jointly. Their councils come up with parochial school tuition and send their kids to college at a rate that defies the poverty and illiteracy of their parents. The small percentage of Zapotec youths in gangs are often exiled to a year in Oaxaca.[137]

As one would expect, the relationship between these communal allegiances and larger social struggles is quite complex.[138] Some researchers argue that broad class solidarity, as expressed through trade unions and political mobilization, is undermined by the profusion of parochial loyalties and the obligations to generate surplus incomes for communal priorities. (Immigrant social networks, as we shall see, tend to compete with each other in the informal labor market rather than with native workers.) In her remarkable study of Latino immigrants on Long Island, anthropologist Sarah Mahler worries that the intimate obligations that bind Salvadorean immigrants to their hometowns also forces them into relentless competition with each other and other Latino immigrants.[139] Carol Zubin from U.C. Berkeley's Labor Center, on the other hand, contrasts the opposite roles of *paesanismo* in two of the most important Southern California labor struggles of the last decade. Thus one of the principal grievances that led 800 workers to strike the American Racing Equipment Company in 1990 was the favoritism shown by foremen to workers from their home village or region. Yet during the explosive 1992 struggle of 4000 drywall workers "the social networks based on immigrants' village of origin [El Maguey in Guanajuato] helped build solidarity for the organizing drive." The *drywalleros,* as they call themselves, defied mass arrests, police brutality, threats of deportation and even an attempt by employers to indict them under the Racketeer Influenced and Corrupt Organizations Act (RICO) to achieve, according to labor journalist David Bacon, "the first union contract won by a grassroots organizing effort in the building trades anywhere in the country since the 1930s."[140]

Immigrant social mobilization is also complicated by the fact that so many immigrants occupy strikingly different class positions in the parallel worlds they move between. The town of San Miguel el Alto in Jalisco, for example, has for years provided a flexible supply of labor for Palm Springs, California. During the busy winter and spring seasons, virtually the entire male population moves north to work in the steakhouses, restaurants, hotels and country clubs of the famous desert resort. To most visitors and residents, the Miguelenses – many of whom hold down two, even three jobs at a time – are simply an efficient, largely invisible army of brown labor. But when they return to Jalisco, their social position metamorphoses. Over the decades the regular remittances from Palm Springs have leveraged some of the migrants into enviable positions of economic security and social prestige. A *Los Angeles Times* correspondent who visited San Miguel el Alto was flabbergasted to find waiters and busboys living in "mansions" and being addressed as "don" by their neighbors.[141] Likewise in the case of the Aguilillans in Redwood City, Rouse shows how they willingly proletarianize themselves in California precisely to prevent the proletarianization of their status in Michoacán where they are small ranchers and farmers.[142]

Transnational migration does not always produce serendipitous results, of course. Immigration researchers contrast the experiences of older cohorts of immigrants, like the veteran Miguelenses and Anguilillans, whose goal has been the recapitalization of their productive property and social position in Mexico, with those of newcomers who have had to come north simply to meet basic consumption needs.[143] In her study of a half-century of labor migration between Napízaro and the San Fernando Valley, Fletcher finds that migration has been transformed from a resource for solidarity into an increasingly divisive force. "Between the 1940s and the mid-1980s migration provided new routes to success for many villagers, and migrant remittances were at times used to further village-wide projects and to further the aims of shared prosperity. However, since the late 1980s, a widening gap in income and changing values in terms of consumption, changing practices in production, severe limits of land,

and declining earnings for migrants in the recession have eroded village unity." The widening class divide in Napízaro is symbolized by the large, gated and often empty *casas de sueños* (dream homes) built by older, more successful immigrants who work in California for most of the year. Meanwhile, their younger and poorer neighbors experience diminishing returns as they attempt to scrape livelihoods together on smallholdings in Michoacán or by selling their labor on street corners in North Hollywood.[144]

There is also evidence that transnational social networks are frequently subsidized by the superexploitation of women.[145] The increasing shift in the social reproductive function of the household from the local family farm to the provision of labor for export generates new disadvantages for women. With so much of the male workforce in California, for example, the women who remain behind in the Aguililla or San Miguel must shoulder even larger burdens of child care, domestic toil and wage labor. Likewise, female immigrants are often shunted into sweatshop apparel or servile house-cleaning jobs that offer the least opportunity for vertical or even horizontal mobility. Although immigration to big US cities may also offer unexpected freedoms to young women (including college educations for Ticuanense girls and more egalitarian households for Dominicanas),[146] immigrant social networks are more typically committed to the enforcement of traditional gender roles. Thus it is not surprising, according to Jacqueline Hagan, that "positive outcomes of enclave economies for men may be enjoyed at the cost of women's opportunities."[147]

Another contradiction inherent in large-scale immigration is the inadvertent remittance of US social problems as well as migradollars to the home community. Given the extreme gradient between the violent streets of the American inner city and the generally peaceful village worlds of rural Mexico or even Central America, this is an ever-present danger. Los Angeles, in particular, has become notorious for exporting its deadly street wars to its transnational suburbs. Thanks to a local law-enforcement strategy that relies upon the mass deportation (usually without trial) of noncitizen gangmembers, thousands of angry, unemployed L.A. youth have been repatriated to Mexico, Belize, El Salvador (4000 alone) and Guatemala. The predictable result has been an epidemic of alien urban violence in often incongruous rural contexts. In the small Salvadorean town of Quezaltepeque (population 13,000), there were nearly a dozen killings in 1997 as a result of a transplanted gang war between *repatriados* of Los Angeles's 18th Street and Mara Salvatrucha sets.

9

FALLING DOWN

Lauriano Avilez was working with a large crew laying concrete for the fourth story of a housing project for Hassidic families in Brooklyn's crowded Williamsburg district. Three months previously, construction had been briefly halted when an OSHA inspector discovered a dangerous overload of concrete blocks on one floor, but work was allowed to resume when the contractor promised to comply with safety regulations. He never did, and as Avilez later told the *New York Times*, "We knew it wasn't stable. The building was not in good condition." Avilez and the others, mostly unemployed carpenters from central Mexico, were troubled by the obvious hazard but were afraid to complain. They had spent too many hungry mornings begging for work in the "slave market" on the corner of Division Street and Bedford Avenue to risk a steady job, so they tried to put the danger out of mind. "We were laying down cement. I didn't even notice. All of a sudden, everything fell, all of it. I was left hanging. I just hung on with my hands."[148]

When paramedics and firefighters arrived they found terrible carnage. The collapse of the overloaded and improperly braced floor had plunged a dozen workers sixty feet to the ground. Those who weren't impaled by reinforcing rods or crushed by falling scaffolding were trapped in rapidly hardening concrete. "You would just see hands and feet in the cement," one rescuer said, "some laying face up, some lying face down. They thought they were drowning. They thought they were being buried alive." In the event, Daniel Eduardo (twenty-two) died on the spot and others were grievously injured. As ambulances removed the victims, some of their *compañeros* vented frustration and anger. "With these jobs, you bust your butt and they want to pay you $6 an hour. It isn't right. The bosses are always rushing us to do the job fast."[149]

This small massacre in November 1999 was followed by another three months later. Fire broke out in a basement sweatshop in a ten-story building in Manhattan's garment district. Smoke quickly filled the stairwell, blocking the escape of employees on the upper floors. "On the eighth floor, a woman working for a dress manufacturer tied one end of white silk around a pillar, tied the other end around her waist, climbed out a window and slid down two floors to the rooftop of an adjacent building, where she scrambled down a fire escape." Other workers attempting to follow her example were not so lucky. On the tenth floor, 42-year-old Benvenito Hernández, employed by a leather manufacturer, lost his grip on a makeshift rope and fell to his death in full view of his horified co-workers. A middle-aged woman was critically injured in another fall. OSHA officials told the *New York Times* that citations were commonly issued in the garment industry for "blocked exits, a lack of fire extinguishers and a lack of escape plans."[150]

Such tragedies shed light not only on the Dickensian underworld of day labor but also on the mechanism by which New York City's Mexican immigrant population ballooned from 100,000 in 1990 to an estimated 350,000 in 1999. As Robert Smith found in his research on the Ticuanense and other Pueblan immigrants, they have tried to create niches for themselves in supersaturated labor markets by becoming "perfect proletarians," living only to work and send money home. In addition to nonunion construction and apparel manufacturing, their reputation for ferocious hard work and long hours has warmly recommended them to Greek restaurateurs and Korean greengrocers, whose own immigrant countrymen are considered too independent and "expect to be treated as members of the family." In a detailed survey, Smith discovered that Mexican grocery helpers took home $180 for a seventy-hour week in 1990 while Korean co-nationals demanded $500. The Mexicans, moreover, stretched their meager earnings through pooled resources and household economies of scale. "In one case, immigrants from one *municipio* in Mexico maintained a virtual monopoly over several SROs in Manhattan – for example, by never officially moving out but replacing one *paisano* with another – and then, as a group, they moved into particular neighborhoods in Queens and the Bronx."[151]

In business-school terms, many Latino immigrants are able to deploy "social capital" to reduce their subsistence costs and thereby subsidize their own superexploitation. This goes part of

the way toward explaining how it has been possible for Latino
urban populations to grow so rapidly during periods when most
US big cities have been undergoing massive deindustrialization.
Immigration foes, of course, contend that the likes of Laureano
Avilez, Daniel Eduardo and Benvenito Hernández have stolen entire crops of jobs from native-born workers. Indeed, one former
Los Angeles Times editorialist used the pages of the *Atlantic Monthly*
to blame the 1992 Rodney King riots on the displacement of Black
labor by recent immigration from Mexico.[152] Others have attributed California's environmental crisis, even the gridlock on its
freeways, to the federal government's alleged failure to control
the border. Similar arguments are heard every day in New York
and Florida.

Academic research, however, has found surprisingly little
documentary evidence that immigrants are supplanting native-
born workers.[153] Thus a recent study of immigrants and domestic
migrants in Los Angeles industry found too little sectoral overlap
between the two groups to constitute any significant arena for
direct competition.[154] A comparative analysis by the same authors
of the five metropolitan areas with the largest foreign-born populations – Los Angeles, San Francisco, Chicago, Miami and New
York – similarly concluded that immigrants typically moved into
employment niches that were either directly created by immigration itself (like ethnic restaurants and small apparel factories) or
abandoned by native workers en route to better jobs in the suburbs. They *replaced,* not displaced the native-born.[155] Even the
controversial 1998 report by RAND analysts Kevin McCarthy and
Georges Vernez – which goes further than many researchers be-

lieve warranted to quantify immigration's negative impact on native-born workers – finds that "immigration has affected the job
opportunities of a relatively small fraction of the California labor
force." They attribute, for example, 16 percent of the job loss and
earnings decline experienced by African-American males without
high school diplomas since the 1970s to the competition of Mexican and Central American immigrants.[156]

If accurate, this is not a negligible effect, but it hardly equals
wholesale ethnic displacement – certainly not on the scale of
European immigrants' catastrophic impact on Black urban opportunity in 1885–1915. (Clearly, as Denton and Massey have re-
minded us, the enduring Black unemployment crisis primarily
arises out of the institutional obstacles – including persistent residential segregation, workplace discrimination, collapsing inner-
city schools and rampant criminalization of Black youth – that
prevent so many poor African-American families from entering
the college-credentialed information economy or following the
white working class out to the job-rich edge cities.)[157] The real
burden of labor immigration, as the National Research Council
concluded after careful study in 1997, is borne by other immigrants.[158] There is a broad consensus among veteran researchers
that Latinos primarily compete either against one another or
against *maquila* workers on the other side of the border. This
competition has grown more darwinian in the slump-then-boom
economy of the 1990s. Clearly there are limits to supply creating
its own demand in otherwise overstocked low-skill labor markets.

In a recent study of Los Angeles County's ethnic populations
commissioned by the Russell Sage Foundation, one author mar-

veled at the "massively growing numbers of Mexican immigrants
... packed into a relatively narrow tier of occupations."[159] While
the initial cohorts of immigrants in the 1960s and 1970s may have
enjoyed considerable success, immigrant economic opportunity
(at least for the bearers of labor-power and not capital) has declined sharply since the mid-1980s.[160] "Economic conditions in
Los Angeles have deteriorated for Mexican immigrants. Economic restructuring simultaneously pulls these immigrants into
the lowest-paid and most easily exploitable jobs and removes the
mobility structures that unskilled newcomers previously used to
get ahead. ... Mexicans and Central Americans seem to have
herded into niches [including gardening, food preparation, house-
cleaning and garment manufacture] that constitute mobility
traps."[161] Another report suggests that deindustrialization in the
early 1990s rendered ethnic resources and social networks less
useful than previously to Mexican newcomers to Los Angeles.[162]

These trends apply to the California economy as a whole. For
their part, McCarthy and Vernez argue that "the pool of low-skill
jobs is shrinking, belying the widespread belief that California's
past 20 to 30 years of 'economic restructuring' expanded the
number of jobs for less-educated workers."[163] A study commissioned by state Senate Majority Leader Richard Polanco established that "Latinos are 28 per cent of the labor force, but account
for only 19 percent of the aggregate wages." (African-Americans,
by contrast, were near parity for their share of the labor-force.)[164]

Declining opportunity was also a principal conclusion of the
recent Binational Study on Migration, a joint Mexican–US research project commissioned by Zedillo and Clinton, which

found that "in 1996, 11 percent of recently arrived families headed by a Mexican-born person had incomes below $5000, compared with 5.5 percent in 1990."[165] Even Cuban-Americans – widely resented by other immigrant groups for their special treatment – have had a more ambiguous experience than their ethnic-success-story stereotype suggests. Through the 1980s at least, their average family income lagged significantly behind the national aver-

Figure 4 Median Wage Income in California, March 1998

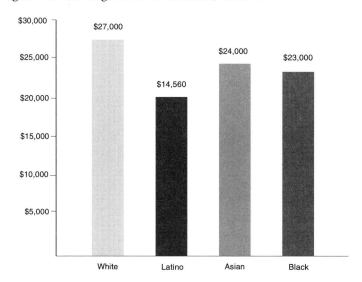

Source: Elías López, Enrique Ramírez and Refugio Rochin, *Latinos and Economic Development in California*, California Research Bureau, Sacramento, Calif. 1999, p.7.

age, while their high school dropout rate soared. As María de los Angeles Torres points out in "Working Against the Miami Myth," "The facts show that while many Cubans did make it, many more did not – despite the unprecedented welfare benefits, English-language classes, university and business loans, and covert CIA money that flowed into South Florida."[166]

Spanish-surname households as a whole are also extraordinarily vulnerable to the business cycle. The early 1990s recession, whose national epicenter was Los Angeles County, devastated the barrios. The median household income of 30 million US Latinos fell by nearly $3000 between 1989 and 1996 – the biggest loss registered by any ethnic group since the Depression.[167] In the same period, the ratio of Latino to Black managerial-professionals (a gauge of relative occupational mobility) slipped from 62 percent to 58 percent despite the faster growth of the Spanish-surname population.[168] Similarly, Latinos have been the last to enjoy the fruits of the subsequent recovery and high-tech-driven boom.[169]

Decreasing returns to Latino immigration (in a hemispheric context where the supply of emigrants will, nonetheless, continue to grow) may seem less worrisome when it is remembered that the rest of the US population is rapidly aging (demographers estimate that by 2040 an astonishing 3.4 million Californians will be older than eighty). Most economists are thus more alarmed about future labor-supply shortages than gluts.[170] The trick will be to unlock the immigrant job ghettoes, at least for second-generation children, by raising education and skill levels en masse, as was done for previous generations by the G.I. Bill and the postwar community college boom. As we shall see in a moment, however, the public schools are systematically failing Latinos. "Only 5 percent of Hispanic immigrants graduate from college," observes the *National Journal's* John Maggs, "all but shutting out millions of other Hispanics from the credentials and skills that are increasingly the means for escaping poverty in America."[171] This is why most national Latino leaders and local elected officials assert that education must be the central battleground in the struggle for equality.

Table 8
Median Household Income Growth, 1980–1995
(Unadjusted Dollars)

Whites	$4845
Blacks	$4576
Latinos	$269

Source: US Bureau of the Census, *Census and You*, November 1996, p. 10.

Yet there is disturbing evidence that even when the dual effects of "imported poverty" and high dropout rates are filtered from income analyses, Latinos at every level of educational qualification are still losing ground in the cyber-economy. Nationally the weekly earnings of Latinos have fallen from 78.7 percent of the national median in 1980 to 69.6 percent in 1998 (see Table 8).[172] Part of this slippage, to be sure, is due to the catastrophic decline of earning ability by the non-college-educated during the 1980s (male Latino high school *graduates*, for example, experienced a loss of $2700) multiplied by Latinos' low college admission rates. But what is surprising is how poorly the more educated strata of Latinos have fared compared to other groups. For the population as a whole, for example, the possession of a junior college degree or the completion of "some college" improved annual income by almost $1000 during the 1980s; Latino men with the same qualifications, however, experienced an erosion of $410.[173]

Data from Southern California are even more dramatic. According to a recent study by James Allen and Eugene Turner of thirty-four different ethnic groups in the greater Los Angeles area (14.5 million residents), US-born Mexican men (Chicanos) have seen their median incomes decline from 81 percent of non-Hispanic white men in 1959 to 61 percent in 1990. For male Mexican immigrants, the fall was from 66 percent to 39 percent; for immigrant females, as compared to white women, from 81 percent to 51 percent.[174] Working with the same census data, UCLA's Paul Ong and Rebecca Morales were startled to discover that "the earnings gap between a highly educated Chicano and highly educated Anglo [in metropolitan Los Angeles] is greater than that between a minimally educated Chicano and minimally educated Anglo."[175] As Cruz Bustamante, then Speaker of the California Assembly, explained to PBS's *NewsHour* in 1997, "In other words, while an Anglo plumber and a Latino plumber may have a 10 percent wage disparity, this disparity is greater between Anglos and Latinos in professional fields such as engineering."[176]

No matter how carefully one fine-tunes the data to control for further differences in age and regional distribution, Latinos have lower returns on education than non-Hispanic whites. Two additional structural variables, in addition to immigration status and education, are necessary to explain why Latinos are losing ground in the economy. One, not surprisingly, is racism. A New York–based study concluded that racial discrimination accounted for at least one-third of the current income gap between Latino and white men (two-thirds in the case of Black males).[177] Secondly, while US-born Latino citizens, like Chicanos and Puerto Ricans, have greater lateral mobility than immigrants within blue-collar and clerical occupations,[178] they too are largely excluded from cutting-edge sectors. Latinos as a whole have benefited far less from the transition to information-based urban economies than have whites. In both New York and Los Angeles, Spanish surnames are conspicuously absent from the major high-wage industries that drive their regional economies in the post–Cold War era: financial services and entertainment production, respectively.

A six-month investigation by the *San Francisco Chronicle* in 1998 also suggests that Latinos are trapped on the wrong side of the "digital divide" by bad schools and rampant job discrimination. After analyzing the employment records of the thirty-three leading Silicon Valley firms and interviewing hundreds of executives, academics and activists, the *Chronicle* concluded that massive underrepresentation of the region's Black and Latino populations in managerial and professional jobs was the result of five factors: 1) the dearth of science and math education in minority-majority schools; 2) failure to enforce federal affirmative action laws ("violators rarely pay fines and are almost never disqualified from gettin government contracts"); 3) job recruiters' neglect of campuses with substantial minority enrollments; 4) absence of supportive "networks" ("there are virtually no top-ranking blacks and Latinos in Silicon Valley to inspire and mentor younger employees"); 5) pervasive racism on a scale that belies that Valley's progressive image.

Table 9
The Digital Divide: Unequal Opportunity in Silicon Valley
(Percentage of the Workforce)

	Bay Area	Silicon Valley*	Oracle[†]	Sun[‡]
white	56	61	73	71
Asian	21	28	20	22
Latino	14	7	3	4
Black	8	4	3	3

* Percentages for 33 major high-tech firms. [†] Redwood Shores, 11, 773 employees.
[‡] Mountain View, 11,385 employees.
Source: *San Francisco Chronicle*, May 4, 1998.

Indeed, some of the worst offenders are cyber-capital icons like Apple, Sun, Adobe, Netscape and Oracle, all of whom have been fined or sued for racial discrimination or failure to meet federal diversity deadlines. Three of the largest firms lacked even of single Latino official or manager. "It is pretty clear," says UC Santa Cruz's Manuel Pastor, "that there's ethnic and occupation segregation going on in Silicon Valley."[179]

Locked out of the "New Economy," it is not surprising that Latinos are also the least likely to profit individually or through group membership from the *fin de siècle* stock market bubble. According to a January 2000 Federal Reserve study, the bottom fifth of Americans, as a result of exploding household debt, actually had fewer assets than in 1995.[180] White median wealth, thanks to real estate and Dow Jones, is now almost ten times that of Latinos: $45,700 versus $4700.)[181]

10

THE PUERTO RICAN TRAGEDY

In the worst-case scenario, many of today's Mexican, Central American and Dominican immigrants may recapitulate the bitter experience of the Puerto Rican diaspora. Puerto Rican poverty, which rebuts the facile claim that citizenship provides a magic carpet for immigrant success,[182] is the spectre that ineluctibly haunts all debates about the future of the Latino metropolis. During the Great Migration from 1946 to 1964, nearly two-fifths of the island's population moved to New York and other eastern seaboard cities. They achieved modest but real economic gains until 1960, when all forward motion ground to a halt. As Clara Rodriguez observes with disquiet: "While other minorities experienced a period of socioeconomic advancement during the 1960s, followed by a phase of limited gains during the 1970s, the Puerto Rican experience is one of continuously growing disadvantage since 1960."[183] Relative to every group except Native Americans (also excluded from any economic benefit during the Vietnam War boom or the Civil Rights era), Puerto Ricans have been losing ground since the inauguration of John F. Kennedy. Thus the proportion of Puerto Rican families with incomes "below one quarter of the median incomes of whites rose from 11% in 1960 to 15% in 1970, 26% in 1980, and 33% in 1985."[184] In 1992 the National Puerto Rican Coalition reported that "Puerto Ricans had the highest poverty rate for individuals in the nation at nearly 40% of the total Puerto Rican population compared to 33% for African Americans, and 14.2% for the population at large."[185]

Puerto Rican downward mobility on the mainland has been aggravated by a jobs catastrophe back home. The 1973 OPEC crisis led to a collapse of many of the capital-intensive, oil-based industries that had been promoted in the 1960s as the island's new economic engine. While the mainland quickly recovered from the OPEC recession, Puerto Rico, despite a massive injection of tax breaks, never regained the lost ground. "The 1980s and early 1990s," according to two leading economic analysts, "were a tempestuous period in Puerto Rico's history, and the sharp fluctuations of these years hit the island with the impact of a hurricane." Unemployment more than tripled and by 1990 an incredible 70 percent of Puerto Ricans twenty-five years of age or younger were living in poverty.[186]

The grim conditions in island *municipios* like Adjuntos (1990 per capita income of $2196) or Guayana (38 percent unemployment) are matched by extreme concentrations of Puerto Rican poverty in some of the East Coast's deindustrialized cores like North Philadelphia, east of Broad Street, where two-thirds of kids are growing up in households earning less than $15,500 per year, or Hartford, the most Puerto Rican city in the country (27.3 percent in 1990), where mean per capita incomes are less than one-third that of the rest of the population.[187] Experts on New York City, meanwhile, vie with one another in citing "singularly alarming statistics" like the decline in Puerto Rican income from two-thirds of the city median in 1960 to barely half by 1990; the increase in Puerto Rican poverty during the 1990s boom; or the abysmal ratio of college graduates in 1999 (only 10 percent of Puerto Ricans over age twenty-five, in contrast to 40 percent of non-Hispanic whites).[188] Others have fretted over why Puerto Rican family structures seemingly collapsed following the election of Ronald Reagan: the share of female-headed households soaring from 34.8 percent in 1980 to 43.9 percent in 1985.[189] More

Figure 5
Unemployment Rates in Puerto Rico, 1940–90

Source: Francisco Rivera-Batiz and Carlos Santiago, *Island Paradox: Puerto Rico in the 1990s*, New York 1996, p. 6.

recent studies have confirmed the negligible dividends earned
from lifetimes of toil in New York's sweated trades: "It takes 15
years for Mexicans and 25 years for Puerto Ricans [in New York
City] to have statistically significant wage gains."[190]

There is surprisingly little academic disagreement about the
causes of this socio-economic disaster. Puerto Rican immigrants
in the 1950s (like many African-American migrants from the
South) were shunted into precisely those traditional urban manufacturing jobs that were massively automated, suburbanized or
exported overseas after 1960. Boricuans were, so to speak, standing on the track when Industrial Restructuring came around the
bend at 100 miles per hour. "The nine cities where the majority of
US Puerto Ricans lived in 1980 lost almost one million manufacturing jobs between 1963 and 1982, representing a 44 percent loss
of manufacturing employment."[191] Robert Suro summarizes a
consensus of research on the recent economic history of New
York City:

> When New York's industrial economy sank, the Puerto Ricans sank
> with it. During the 1970s, family income for Puerto Rican New York-
> ers dropped by 18% in real terms, while whites, blacks, and other
> Hispanics experienced gains. ... To make matters worse for Puerto
> Ricans, the losses in income were five times greater when the head
> of the household was born on the mainland, compared with those
> born on the island. The second generation was just entering the
> workforce, only to find the rug pulled out from under it. Their pov-
> erty was born and bred in New York.[192]

Disturbingly, the very institutions that emancipated earlier immigrant groups from the sweatshops betrayed Puerto Ricans. José

Sanchez reminds us that two-thirds of New York's Puerto Rican households in 1959 had at least one union card-holder – most likely a member of the International Ladies Garment Workers Union. The ILGWU's autocratic leader, David Dubinsky, came under much fire from civil rights activists in the 1960s for his refusal to struggle for elementary rank-and-file demands or share power with his increasingly Black and Puerto Rican membership. "Entry-level jobs that had historically served as avenues for advancement to higher paying and more secure jobs for earlier immigrants were recast as permanent low-wage positions and this was accomplished with the consent of the ILGWU ... The real earnings of the rank-and-file members ... mostly Puerto Rican and African-American women, declined below the poverty level for New York City families between 1960 and 1965."[193] Sanchez argues that Dubinsky also prevented Puerto Ricans from using the union's powerful political arm, the Liberal Party, as an effective instrument of empowerment:

> Puerto Ricans were abused and manipulated as members of the Liberal Party. The Liberal Party, for instance, blocked Puerto Ricans from leadership positions within the party, ignored the Puerto Rican community's need for elected representation, supported the growth of the municipal workforce at the expense of manufacturing and, more importantly, campaigned for lower minimum wages in the state. These actions not only weakened Puerto Ricans politically but dampened their wages and undermined their bargaining position with employers. Thus, while the Liberal Party paraded around as a workers' party, nothing could be further from the truth as far as Puerto Ricans were concerned.[194]

Unfortunately, there is growing evidence that many poor Latino immigrants (apart from Cubans) who have arrived since 1980 are becoming enmired in the same poverty trap that has destroyed the dreams of mainland Puerto Ricans. (Again, the 1990–93 recession was a structural watershed.) The social destruction wrought in Latino inner-city neighborhoods by Reagan/Bush/Clinton-era disinvestment in urban educational and welfare safety nets, following on the heels of deindustrialization, has been enormous.[195] Researchers at the Dominican Studies Institute, for example, report that "the decline of manufacturing as a sector of employment has had a devastating impact on Dominican workers, especially women." Despite the stereotype of a Dominican *bodega* on every corner in upper Manhattan, Dominicans are on the verge of displacing Puerto Ricans as the poorest major ethnic group in the city with 36 percent in poverty and only 9 percent self-employed (mainly as micro-entrepreneurs).[196] New York's burgeoning but profoundly underdog Mexican population, as we have seen, struggles to survive in the benthic layer of the economy: working as busboys in Greek restaurants, risking their lives in gypsy construction, illegally selling candy in subway stops, or hustling flowers at street corners.[197] On Long Island, similarly threadbare Central American immigrants – many of whom were laid off during the defense industry downsizing of 1990–93 – expressed to Sarah Mahler narratives of disillusionment: "Their portrayals of their lives in America are full of deceit, dejection, marginalization and exploitation."[198]

The 1986 Immigration Reform Act (IRCA), moreover, institutionalized unprecedented extremes of economic and social marginality. While 2.5 million previously undocumented immigrants gained legal rights to work, and, potentially, to citizenship, several million others who failed to qualify for amnesty or who arrived after the deadline, became criminalized pariahs ("underneath the underdog," as Charlie Mingus once put it). "For my informants," Mahler asserts, "IRCA resulted in indentured servitude to their employers and a terror of discovery."[199] Their job options have been restricted to the most shadowy and exploitative recesses of the urban economy, including apparel home work, itinerant day labor and street-vending. And they are increasingly likely to be homeless or housed in illegal shanty-towns like those tucked away in the back canyons of northern San Diego County, where Guatemalan and Mixtec laborers live clandestinely a few hundred yards from $750,000 ocean-view homes.

Where they are more visible, as in street-corner labor markets in edge cities and exurbs across the country, undocumented workers face a nativist hysteria that frequently rises to an occult pitch. (As Tony Hay, chairman of the Putnam County [New York] Legislature, ranted to the *Times*: "The World Trade Center blew up, planes are blown out of the sky. I'm not saying it's Latinos, but they're all immigrants. The West Nile virus, they laugh at me, but we don't know where that came from. If Saddam Hussein shaved his mustache and spoke Spanish, he could be here and stand on the streets of Brewster. Muammar Quaddafi, he could come here!")[200] In response to such complaints, the INS is systematically subpoenaing personnel records in what it has identified as the major geosectoral concentrations of undocumented labor – janitors in the Bay Area, meat-packing in Nebraska and Iowa, hotel workers in San Diego, and apple-packers in Washington – and calling in those with suspicious identification for interviews. Thousands, as a result, have had to flee their jobs and homes: including, as labor journalist David Bacon discovered in Omaha, the key activists in a drive to organize non-union packing plants. An INS spokesperson gloated over Operation Vanguard's success in words that might have come out of the mouth of Slobodan Milosevic: "We will remove the magnet of jobs. We will clean up one industry and turn the magnet down a bit, and then go on to another industry, and another, and another."[201]

11

EDUCATION GROUND ZERO

It is traditional in the United States to accord education quasi-omnipotence in determining individual and group futures. Elaborate mythologies are woven around immigrant ethnic groups, like Jews, who supposedly attained socio-economic nirvana through their love of education, forgetting that their path to the suburbs lay not just via De Witt Clinton High and CCNY but, equally, through Sidney Hillman's Amalgamated Clothing Workers and Morris Hillquit's Socialist Party. Likewise for Latinos, as we have seen, the relationship between bad schools and bad jobs is far more complex than usually portrayed, particularly when employers value the diplomas of different groups unequally. Still, it was an understatement in 1997 when President Clinton recognized the 30 percent dropout rate among Latino high school students (versus 8 percent for whites and 13 percent for African-Americans) as nothing short of a "national crisis."[202]

In an economy where all the good jobs (even for police officers

and plumbers) seemingly demand at least fourteen years of education, nearly half of Spanish-surname residents aged twenty-five
or older in New York City lack a high school diploma, as do 55
percent of adult Latinos in Massachusetts and 58 percent of Mexican immigrants in Los Angeles.[203] If part of this educational deficit is "imported," US educational institutions are doing little to
raise the qualifications of Latinos to the level of other groups. In
California, even third-generation Chicanos (most of whom don't
speak Spanish) have a high-school attrition rate nearly three times
higher than that of their Anglo peers, while Puerto Rican kids in
New York have only marginally lowered a catastrophic dropout
rate that peaked at 62 percent in the mid-1980s.[204] And, distressingly, inter-ethnic differentials in college attendance have wid-
ened, not decreased, over time (see Table 10). Enrollment figures,
moreover, are misleadingly optimistic since Latinos, as in high
school, drop out of college in appallingly large numbers. In New
York, for example, almost half of Latino and Black students (or a
staggering three-quarters of Puerto Ricans in CUNY) leave college within the first two years.[205] Young Latinos, as a result, are
massively failing to obtain the admission ticket to the virtual
world of 21st-century capitalism. Arizona, for example, has become a leading high-tech state with an economy powered by Mo-
torola and other "silicon desert" firms, yet less than 5 percent of
its 1 million Latino residents possess a college degree.[206]

The Latino educational crisis is rooted in a vicious circle of
family poverty and declining national commitment to big city
school systems. A major study of the causes of Latino school-
leaving, based on interviews with 700 dropouts in San Antonio,

pointed to the "lack of bilingual and English as a Second Language programs, the concentration of Hispanics in high-poverty
schools, lack of teacher preparation and low expectations for Hispanic students among teachers, administrators and society as a
whole."[207] In addition, as every inner-city high school counselor
can testify, there are intense pressures on immigrants' teenage
children (often the only citizens in the household) to supplement
family incomes as soon as possible. Similarly, many families of the
working poor pursue the classic strategy of subsidizing one
child's education by sacrificing the schooling of others.

Table 10
College Enrollment of 18- to 24-Year-Olds
(Percent)

	1980	1990
Whites	20.8	35.9
Blacks	15.6	27.1
Asians	30.3	55.1
Latinos	14.2	22.9

Source: Marcelo Siles, *Income Differentials in the US: Impact on Latino
Socio-Economic Development,* JSRI Working Paper No. 33, Julian
Samora Research Institute, East Lansing, Mich. 1997, p. 5.

Latinos also face innumerable obstacles in returning to education as adults. Long work hours, together with overwhelming
household responsibilities, a nationwide dearth of English-liter-
acy classes, and (conversely) the absence of vocational/profes-
sional education in Spanish, make it very difficult for Latino
adults to upgrade their skills or acquire English proficiency. Soar-

ing tuition in community and state college systems like California's (which were once free) have also priced out thousands of potential poor students. Likewise the armed forces have been far less successful in providing last-resort education and job skills to Latinos than to previous generations of African-Americans and poor whites. As the National Council of La Raza recently reported, Latinos are both underrepresented in the military by nearly a third (relative to their proportion of the civilian workforce) and "disproportionately concentrated in the lowest pay grades, with the lowest level of responsibilities and fewest opportunities."[208]

Meanwhile, big city school systems, with shockingly few exceptions, have become national scandals. The three largest – New York, Los Angeles and Chicago – are terminally ill and unlikely to survive the next decade in their present forms. The present crisis goes back as far as the first wave of white flight in the 1960s but clearly deepened during the 1970s when battles over school integration fueled backlashes (like California's notorious Proposition 13) against property tax–based funding of public education. In Los Angeles and elsewhere, aging white voters (still a majority of the electorate if a minority of the population) have consistently voted down school bonds for minority-majority public schools.[209] Continuing federal Title I subsidies to inner-city education have largely failed to make up for the favoritism shown by suburban-majority state legislatures toward new schools in edge-city growth belts. Moreover, the resegregation of schools during the 1990s, in the wake of further white flight (from both cities and public education) and the federal courts' rulings against man dated integration, have affected Latino children even more than African-Americans (see Table 11). According to Harvard University's Civil Rights Project (using 1997 data), "nationwide, nearly 70 percent of black students and 75 percent of Latinos attend schools that are predominantly black, Latino or Native American."[210]

Table 11
Resegregating US Schools
(Percentage of the Pupils in 90%–100% Minority Schools)

	Blacks	Latinos
1968–69	64.3	23.1
1972–73	38.7	23.3
1980–81	33.2	28.8
1986–87	32.5	32.2
1991–92	33.9	34.0
1996–97	35.0	35.4

Source: Adapted from Megan Twohey, "Desegregation Is Dead," *National Journal*, 18 September 1999, p. 2619.

California, of course, has been ground zero for Latino hopes of an educational breakthrough, and nowhere has white disinvestment in urban schools produced more calamitous results. "Between 1970 and 1997," as the school population shifted from an Anglo majority to a Latino plurality, "spending per pupil in California fell more than 15 percent relative to spending in the rest of the country."[211] As long as the majority of the baby boom were still of school age, California's public schools were a gold standard for the rest of the country. With a booming defense economy offering good jobs to so many otherwise poorly educated white migrants of the Depression era, there was a general willingness to finance quality schools that opened college doors to the sons and daughters of the *Grapes of Wrath*. Now, in the wake of Proposition 13 and the "browning" of older school systems, K-through-12 education in California ranks rock bottom with Mississippi with the lowest fourth grade reading scores in the nation. (Only 18 percent of kids achieved proficiency in the 1994 National Assessment of Educational Progress exams.) Mississippi, however, is at least trying to improve its schools: in a recent *Education Week* scoreboard it was awarded "C plus" for adequacy of education funding while California received a humiliating "F".[212]

Whereas a generation ago the key index of inequality between rich and poor schools would have been class size, today it is teacher quality. "Among school resources," the Public Policy Institute of California explains, "the level of teacher experience and the percentage of teachers without a full credential are the variables most strongly related to student outcomes."[213] A widely discussed 1999 study, funded by the Center for the Future of Teaching and Learning, attributes much of California schools' distress to the poor quality of instruction: more than one in ten classrooms are staffed by teachers with emergency credentials who do not meet the state's minimal certification requirements. Some 1 million of California's 5.7 million public school kids were in schools with "so many underqualified teachers as to make these schools dysfunctional." "Students who score in the bottom quartile of reading achievement in third grade are five times as likely as students scoring in the top quartile to have underqualified teachers. These are the students who, if they don't learn to read soon, will be unable to perform well in any subject area." Not surprisingly, teacher quality is so skewed between white-suburban versus minority-urban or minority-rural districts – for example, one quarter of schools have fully qualified staffs while another half have 20 percent or more unqualified – that the principle of a "common education" has become a bad joke.[214]

This is especially true in the biggest Latino school district in the country: Los Angeles Unified. On the one hand, three out of four new-hire teachers in the district lack qualifications; on the other, a recent self-study, based on standardized test scores, concluded that "more than two-thirds of eighth graders would be flunked if social promotions were fully ended."[215] Dispirited, underqualified and increasingly temporary teachers are sent as cannon-fodder into the district's massively overcrowded and underequipped schools, while dedicated, fully credentialed colleagues are siphoned off by the higher salaries and state-of-the-art teaching environments in elite private or new-suburb public schools. As a result, "teaching in many urban areas has become a temporary job like waiting on tables while looking for that big break in show business." The *Los Angeles Times* recently described the misery of one of these ill-prepared "temp teachers" in a majority Latino and Black middle school in Southcentral Los Angeles:

> An aspiring screenwriter, she had never taught before and received only five days of training in things such as how to record attendance. When she arrived at the school this fall, she wasn't even given a lesson guide. She had 10 books for 40 students. She's been all but ignored by the principal and her more experienced colleagues. Stu-

dents curse at her and threaten her. ... Once she taught an entire period in a classroom with blood on the floor and desks – from a student fight. Janitors had been called but didn't show up. "It's the most horrible, horrible place I've ever been in my entire life," she said. Still, she needs the job, so she didn't want her name used. She hopes to stick it out until at least after Christmas, but she's not confident she can. Then, the revolving door will turn and some other aspirant will take her place.[216]

12

DISABLING SPANISH

Last year our government spent nearly $8 billion abusing chil-
dren. Deprive a child of an education. Handicap a young life
outside the classroom. Restrict social mobility. If it came at the
hand of a parent it would be called child abuse. At the hand of
our schools and funded primarily by state and local government, it's called bilingual education.

US English ad in *Time,* March 20, 1995

The ultimate betrayal of Latino children is the demagoguery that
asserts that their main "handicap" is speaking Spanish. Whereas
the rest of the world recognizes that bilingualism is an invaluable
comparative advantage is a globalized economy, Spanish skills are
treated in US schools, frequently even by Latino educators, as a learning disability. Moreover, bilingual education has recently become the
target of a cynical national crusade that vilifies it and its supporters
as the principal cause of Latino educational failure. Nativists like Pat
Buchanan and Pete Wilson, as well as compulsory Americanizers
closer to the moderate-right political mainstream, are investing heav-

ily in Spanish-bashing as a lucrative wedge issue for the 2000s. Under
the deceitful slogan of "English for Children" they are attempting to
build a linguistic and cultural Fortress America.

Most Americans are deeply confused about the relationship
between language, nationality and citizenship. Despite the widespread belief that the Pilgrim Fathers or the Continental Congress legislated English as an official language, linguistic diversity
flourished in the United States (partly thanks to local control of
education) until the First World War, when the Midwest's thriving
German-language schools and daily newspapers came under attack from xenophobic legislatures and mobs. The first state "English Only" amendments, like Nebraska's in 1920, were specifically
targeted at bilingual German-American communities, which they
compulsorily monoglotized over the next generation. The sub-
sequent, often coercive, "Americanization" of second-generation
immigrant children during the New Deal and early Cold War eras
made language chauvinism almost redundant as a separate issue
or movement.[217]

Following a cautious renaissance of local experimentation
with bilingualism in the 1960s and early 1970s (Dade County, for
example, became officially bilingual in 1973), English Only was
cloned back to life in Miami in 1980 as part of the angry backlash
against the Mariel exodus from Cuba. It quickly spread virally to
California under the sponsorship of Republican Senator (and famous linguist) Samuel Hayakawa, who in turn introduced an
English Language Amendment in Congress the following year.
Although Hayakawa's national amendment was a stillborn publicity stunt, "Official English" became a lightning rod for white anxi-

eties in California and was tacked onto the state constitution with
the support of 73 percent of Anglo voters in 1986 – despite its
violation of the 1849 Treaty of Guadalupe Hidalgo, which implic-
itly guaranteed the status of Spanish in the conquered borderlands of Mexico. (Interestingly, in a state where Blacks and Latinos are often depicted as political foes, 56 percent of
African-American voters rejected Proposition 63.) White voters in
Arizona and Florida followed suit in 1988, as have legislatures in
Indiana, South Dakota and eight Deep South states.[218]

A permanent, well-endowed lobby – US English – was established in Washington and initially attracted the support of old-
fashioned Americanizers like Linda Chavez (the Madame Chiang
Kai-shek of Latino conservatism) and Walter Cronkite. They
eventually resigned when leaked documents revealed an organization steeped in *herrenvolkish* bigotry. For example, the group's
founder, Dr. John Tanton, likes to terrify supporters with apoca-
lyptic Aryan rhetoric that might have been lifted from the pages
of the *Turner Diaries*:

> To govern is to populate. In this society where the majority rules,
> does this hold? Will the present majority peaceably hand over its
> political power to a group that is simply more fertile? Perhaps this is
> the first instance in which those with their pants up are going to get
> caught by those with their pants down! ... As whites see their power
> and control over their lives declining, will they go quietly into the
> night? Or will there be an explosion?[219]

Such indiscrete ventings of white supremacism temporarily
paralyzed anti-Spanish as a mainstream cause. In addition, many
Republican strategists were appalled by Pete Wilson's scorched-

earth tactics in California as he openly recruited the dregs of the militia fringe to help repel the Brown Invasion ("They Keep Coming – 2,000,000 Illegal Immigrants" intoned a notorious television ad endorsed by Wilson). One of the governor's sharpest critics was Ron Unz, a whiz-kid millionaire with a physics PhD who financed his own emergence from obscurity in 1994 when he took 30 percent of the Republican primary vote away from Wilson. Intellectually, Palo Alto–based Unz is the love-child of Mickey Kaus and Thomas Sowell, the *New Republic* and *Commentary*, not the traditional California right. He "likes immigrants" but wants to see them quickly assimilated without undue state interference in the marketplace of talent. Accordingly, he opposed Proposition 187 (to punish undocumented immigrants) in 1994 almost as vigorously as he campaigned in favor of Proposition 209 (to end affirmative action) in 1996. Moreover, in the best Silicon Valley tradition, he has come up with an invention that he hopes will reframe the national debate about immigration and multiculturalism (and help pave his own way to political office).

Unz-designed Proposition 227 ("English for Children"), which became California law in June 1998 despite the vehement opposition of 63 percent of Latino voters, is an ingenious repackaging of English Only as a rescue package to bring immigrant children into the mainstream. With only sixty days to develop a new curriculum, schools were ordered to transfer immigrant kids into "structured English immersion" for a maximum of a year, then – regardless of proficiency – into regular English-only classrooms. Although parents are allowed to apply for waivers for alternative (including bilingual) language programs, the option has been poorly advertised and many working parents are unable, as required, to apply in person during school hours. On the other hand, "English for Children" virtually criminalizes teachers who continue to assist unwaivered students in Spanish: they are now liable to personal lawsuits as well as termination. The same two-thirds majority requirement that earlier carved Proposition 13 and "three strikes" into California granite makes Prop. 227 equally unrepealable.

The exact content of the proposition, however, is less important than the barrage of obfuscation laid down in its behalf. Prominent Latino neoconservatives like Jaime Escalante of *Stand and Deliver* fame and Pepperdine University's Gregory Rodriguez praised Unz as the authentic voice of the long-suffering majority of California Latino families. Voters were given the impression that most English-learners, over the opposition of their own parents, were being forcibly warehoused in bilingual programs long ago discredited by educational researchers. Thus prevented from acquiring all-important English skills, they were inevitably demoralized and many, as a result, dropped out of school. To provide a motive for such criminal neglect, the more rabid publicists for Prop. 227 advanced the idea of a sinister conspiracy of "left-wing multiculturalists and ethnic nationalists" (Gregory Rodriguez). "Powerful forces," writes *New Times* columnist Jill Stewart, "see Proposition 227 as a direct threat to their vision of a separate Spanish world in California."

> The last thing this crowd wants is to train Mexican-American immigrant children how to read and write in English like native-born Americans, as Proposition 227 envisions. To allow that would be to admit that the multi-billion-dollar "bilingual-industrial complex" of

publishers, consultants, trainers, and college theorists who urged
that immigrant children be placed in Spanish has spawned disaster.
The bilingual industry would finally have to face the fact that it
destroyed the opportunities and equal chances of three or four million children who were denied English skills in California classrooms
during the past twenty years.[220]

The systematic rebuttal of these calumnies, unfortunately, has
largely taken place in professional educational journals outside
the hearing range of the voting public. "The 'failure' of bilingual
education," Stephen Krashen laments, "has reached the status of
urban myth. Even those who were opposed to California's Proposition 227 assumed that bilingual education had serious problems.
The research, however, does not say this at all."[221] What it does
say is that 70 percent of limited English proficient kids in California in 1978 were not in bilingual classes (some content instruction
in Spanish) at all, and that no data currently exists to support a
correlation between bilingual methods and high drop-out rates.
Likewise many of the star examples of English immersion cited
by Proposition 227 supporters, including programs in El Paso and
McAllen, Texas, and Orange County, California, have large bilingual components.[222] So do many of the so-called structured immersion programs (particularly those based on the Québec
model) analyzed in a widely praised 1996 article by C. Rossell and
K. Baker: indeed, as the California State Library's Research Bureau observed, "This study highlights the inconsistent use of program labels."[223]

At the end of the day, the false antinomy between immersion
and bilingual methods is a construct of politicians like Unz, not

teachers or academic researchers. In an authoritative 1997 report, the National Academy of Sciences forcefully rejected the fallacy that "one size fits all" in early English aquisition.[224] Several studies, for example, suggest that immersion works well for young children, three to seven years old, with "neurologically open windows of opportunity for language skill," but is less suited for older students tackling more abstract learning content. Moreover, the success or failure of either method largely depends upon the overall quality of the learning environment: the unification of language and content in the curriculum, teacher training, class size, liaison with parents, home print resources, and so on.[225] But "most students in bilingual programs are working-class students who do not have access to resources for educational success."[226]

> The English-only advocates have successfully made many people believe that bilingual education, of any form, is damaging to limited English proficiency students, badly delivered, and fundamentally un-American. But many of the problems with bilingual education come not so much from the viability of the concept as from its implementation. Many schools that offer bilingual education do not have nearly enough certified, trained and competent staff to deliver quality bilingual education. Many school districts have resorted to hiring bilingual aides who are not trained in bilingual education and do not have education degrees beyond a high-school diploma. These aides teach three-fifths of the limited English proficient children in high-poverty schools.[227]

Educational equity remains the bottom-line issue for Latinos, but it was completely occluded by the bilingual controversy. Proposition 227's opponents, stunned by the ferocity of the attack, hardly emerged from their bunkers, and, when they did, it was to do battle on terms largely defined by Unz: how best to accelerate student transition to the English-only mainstream. Bilingual classrooms were defended only as a means of remediating the English deficit. The alternative of a bilingual mainstream never became an item in the debate except as a scarecrow for white fear. Yet a recent study of six high schools in California and Arizona that have been most successful in preparing limited English proficiency students for college found that comprehensive biculturalism was the decisive variable. "In most of the schools, most of the teachers learned and spoke Spanish and were in close communication with the parents of their students. In one school, the Latino principal did away with the remedial programs, including the bilingual program, and created a bilingual program that was rigorous and included college preparatory courses, and quadrupled the size of the bilingual teaching staff."[228]

These schools are examples of "developmental bilingual education" (DBE), which uses the resources of family and cultural community to develop true bilingualism rather than just a transition to English. (Some researchers contrast the "additive" approach of DBE, which validates first language skills and cognitive abilities, to the "subtractive" model of most immersion and "bilingual" programs which aim simply to substitute English for Spanish as rapidly as possible.)[229] As Wayne Thomas and Virginia Collier have eloquently argued, the entire debate about English acquisition is absurdly upside-down. "Why do US schools rely so much on remediation for students who are culturally and linguistically diverse? We assess new arrivals from a deficit perspective, looking for what's missing. And when we find that students have little or no English, we send them to a specialist to be 'fixed.' Yet these students often arrive with a wealth of life experiences, including age-appropriate thinking, richly expressed in primary language." In the best DBE schools, bilingual methods are integral components of a larger, community-affirming Freireian pedagogy. "In this type of enrichment program, active parent-school partnerships build on 'funds of knowledge' in the community. Instead of perceiving the home and the community as barriers to learning, the school uses the community as a wealth of resources to create a meaningful bicultural curriculum." Moreover, Thomas and Collier claim that "the growing research base on long-term outcomes clearly demonstrates that ESL [English as a Second Language] pullout is the least effective model, whereas DBE is the most effective."[230]

Unfortunately, most Latino elected officials are too timid or solicitous of non-Hispanic voters to openly champion the idea that bilingualism is the solution not the problem. DBE has prestigious academic support but few charismatic or well-heeled political advocates with a pass-key to the media: which is why most parents, including Latinos, have never heard of its successes. Unz, on the other hand, is a juggernaut on the move. His bombastic website – "One Nation/One California" – promises that he will fight on until Spanish and other alien tongues are purged from every classroom in the United States. His "English for the Children Arizona" initiative is on the 2000 ballot (despite militant "Unz Go Home!" demonstrations in Tucson), and supporters in other states are gearing up new anti-Spanish crusades. More ominously, there is growing interest in Congress in scuttling the Bilingual Education Act or, at least, amending it to restrict instruction to English only. The trend toward a national Prop. 227 was reinforced in 1998 when Education Secretary Richard Riley endorsed a three-year maximum for federally funded bilingual programs although most experts feel that four to six years are required to acquire proficiency in academic English.[231]

There is, of course, a certain deja vu to the current backlash against Spanish. California enjoyed the benefits of English-only education from 1872 to 1967 – which is one reason why only half of 18- to 24-year-old Chicanos in 1960 had even completed eighth grade. Many Latino leaders worry that Ron Unz and his patronizing supporters are trying to turn the clock backwards. "The elimination of bilingual education," warns Dr. Juan Andrade, "will only increase the number of Latino students at risk, and virtually ensure their illiteracy in two languages. Proposition 227 was not about 'English for the Children.' It was about re-institutionalizing discrimination and legalizing the deprivation of knowledge and educational opportunity. This proposition sanctions the rejection of Latino culture and our language in society and in the public schools."[232]

13

WHO WILL FEED THE DRAGON?

In the face of increasing income and educational inequalities, the search for greater economic and political power has become an imperative for Spanish-surname urban populations. Latinos, all political pundits agree, are the sleeping dragon of US politics. With the exception of Cuban-Americans in Miami, they are grotesquely disfranchised in every major metropolitan area. More than 7 million adults out of a national Latino voting-age population of 18.4 million in 1996 lacked citizen rights. As a result, many urban constituencies resemble eighteenth-century British "rotten boroughs" with tiny effective electorates. In one Los Angeles council district, for example, more than two-thirds of adults are noncitizens and in a recent election only 2 percent of the population voted. Likewise in New York City, only 5 percent of 1,468,876 non–Puerto Rican Latinos voted in the last citywide election.[233] As a result, Latinos are extraordinarily under-represented in public office in most states. In Dallas, for example, where Spanish-surname kids constitute 51 percent of the student population, Latinos have exactly one school board member while whites (12 percent of students) have five.[234] Nationally, Latinos (with a population almost equal to African-Americans) held a mere 18 seats in the 106th Congress (versus 37 Black seats) and none in the Senate.

This long history of political marginality is, however, finally coming to an end. The recent wave of immigrant-bashing, including Proposition 187 in California and the demagogic presidential campaigns of Ross Perot and Patrick Buchanan in 1996, have produced a powerful Latino electoral riposte.[235] Like the great 1928 surge in urban Catholic and Jewish votes stimulated by the growth of the Ku Klux Klan in the north, the new nativism has spurred citizenship and voter registration efforts. Indeed, the naturalization process has almost collapsed under the weight of 2.5 million Asian and Latino applicants. For Mexicans, moreover, the path to the US voting booth has been eased by the Mexican Congress's recent decision to allow dual citizenship. In 1997, an astonishing 255,000 Mexican immigrants became US citizens, breaking the previous single-nation naturalization record of 106,626 Italians in 1944.[236]

As a result, the 1996 and 1998 elections were a watershed for Latino political hopes. Although the overall vote in 1996 declined by 8 percent in one of the lowest presidential election turnouts in American history, the Latino share rose by a spectacular 16 percent (and registration by 28 percent). If Latinos still constitute only 7 percent of the active electorate, their votes are strategically concentrated in the four states – California, Texas, Florida and New York – that control the Electoral College.[237] In New York

City and Los Angeles, moreover, Latino turnout in 1996 surpassed the Black vote for the first time in history.[238] It is generally
conceded that high Latino turnouts enabled Clinton to beat Dole
in Florida and normally bedrock Republican Arizona, where a
(pre-Unz) "English Only" initiative outraged Mexican residents
and allowed Democrats to carry the state for the first time since
1948.[239] Meanwhile, Governor Pete Wilson's shrill crusade against
immigrants in California helped raise the Latino vote from 7 percent to 14 percent of the total. In the presidential election, Clinton did spectacularly well in Los Angeles's San Gabriel Valley, the
largest single concentration of Latino votes in the nation. In 1998
one of the Valley's representatives in Sacramento, liberal stalwart
Antonio Villaraigosa, succeeded Cruz Bustamente (who became
lieutenant-governor) as the Speaker of the California Assembly.
Even more shocking for old-fashioned conservatives was the de-
feat of ultra-right-wing Orange County congressman Robert
Dornan by Latina Democrat Loretta Sanchez, narrowly in 1996
and overwhelmingly in 1998.

In 2000, Latinos are projected to cast one out of eight votes in
California and one out of five in Texas.[240] As a result, every major
presidential candidate except Pat Buchanan has eagerly boned up
on his high school Spanish, with George W. Bush, who has point-
edly refrained as governor of Texas from incendiary attacks on
immigrant welfare or bilingual education, boasting that he will
steal the Latino vote from Al Gore. (Boy Bush's repeated claim,
however, that "I got nearly fifty percent of the Hispanic vote" in
the 1998 Texas election seems to be patently untrue: he actually
received somewhere between 37 percent and 39 percent.)[241] Yet

Latinos' arrival at a strategic position in national and local politics is bittersweet at best. The translation of demographic strength into electoral clout will remain excruciatingly slow, and even in the "breakthrough year" of 1996, only 4.3 million out of 11.2 million eligible Spanish-surname citizens actually voted.[242]

Low turnouts may in part reflect the shortage of visible rewards conferred by electoral mobilization. The wheels of nonideological mass politics have been traditionally greased by the feedback of material and symbolic power. Not surprisingly, groups whose turnout earns or defends visible progress – like the Irish, Jews and Cubans – have high participation rates, while ethnic groups whose captive votes produce few advantages to themselves – likes Poles and Puerto Ricans – have notorious reputations for low turnout. One doesn't have to be a pavlovian or primitive functionalist to grasp that the current drought of redistributable resources in urban politics has a deterrent impact on voter mobilization. Latinos and Asians, after all, have the bad luck to be repopulating American big cities during an epoch of maximum fiscal disengagement by senior levels of government. Between 1977 and 1985, for example, the federal contribution to municipal budgets slumped from 19 percent to 9 percent in New York City, 18 percent to 2 percent in Los Angeles, and 27 percent to 15 percent in Chicago.[243] Suburb-dominated state legislatures, meanwhile, have stubbornly refused to make up the shortfall. They prefer instead to jettison social mandates, end welfare, close hospitals, reduce public employment, and shift revenues to edge suburbs.

As a result, ethnic breakthroughs in city politics (Miami being a partial exception) no longer deliver the same kinds of spoils as they did in past. In the most extreme cases Latino majorities simply inherit wreckage. The pride and excitement of electing Spanish-surname officials quickly yields to disillusionment and demobilization when electoral euphoria collides with the mean fiscal realities of local government. This is more or less what has happened in the archipelago of aging industrial suburbs southeast of downtown Los Angeles where Chicanos have won city council majorities from 1992 (the locally famous "Bell Gardens revolution") onward. In the fifteen- or even twenty-year gap between the emergence of Latino demographic majorities in the 1970s and the election of Latino city governments in the 1990s, real political competition virtually disappeared as cabals of "good ole boys" manipulated the fears of elderly white voters (a majority of the electorate even when they constituted less than 10 percent of the population) to entrench their control over city budgets and redevelopment agencies. They shaped a plantation politics of town bosses and life-long councilmembers, whose incarnations included the Huey Long–like kingship of City Manager Claude Booker in Bell Gardens and the politbureau-like regime of the "big five" on the Huntington Park City Council. When the "revolution" came, their Chicano successors were stunned to discover that civic fiscal resources had been systematically squandered and that the new majorities were now saddled with huge bonded debts for generally worthless redevelopment initiatives. Voter morale waned as it became clear that "empowerment" meant little more than a Spanish surname on the paychecks to the police and the municipal creditors.[244]

Ultimately there is a danger that the same dismal scenario could play itself out in the City of Los Angeles. As Latinos begin to acquire majority power in the early 2000s (the retiring Speaker of the California Assembly, Antonio Villaraigosa, is already a declared candidate for mayor), the scope for ameliorative politics will be largely defined by social investment decisions made during the 1980s and 1990s. Apart from jobs (and the civil service workforce is essentially frozen in place), the vital public resources for the working poor are education, healthcare and transit. In each instance, the future has been looted in advance. Los Angeles's "Red Line" subway – one of the great public-works disasters in US history – has devoured a generation's worth of transit investment while failing to build an extension to the Eastside and beggaring the bus system upon which most people of color depend. Likewise the school board, faced with the nation's worst crisis of classroom space, has managed to build the most expensive high school in American history over a potentially explosive natural gas deposit that may preclude its ever being used. (In an extraordinary vote of no-confidence in itself, the embattled school district elected to bring in the Army Corps of Engineers to manage new construction.)[245] And, in a metropolitan area where more than a third of Latinos lack health insurance, fiscally strapped county government, against fierce Eastside opposition, is closing or downsizing critical hospital facilities.

Although the electoral guillotine is finally reaping revenge on the school board and federal investigators are crawling over the carcass of the Metropolitan Transportation Authority, the damage to the social infrastructure is colossal. Billions in scarce tax dollars have been squandered to produce little more than ruins and holes in the ground. The only winners have been a handful of giant construction multinationals, their five-star law firms and political henchmen. As a final bad joke on the future, white business and homeowner elites (including key organizers of anti-immigrant Proposition 187) have started a well-financed secession drive in the San Fernando Valley, claiming that the recent fiascos have shown Los Angeles to be "ungovernable." (Activists in the Latino-majority east Valley have retaliated by threatening a subsecession of their own).[246]

14

BROKEN RAINBOWS

Exactly as some Reagan strategists had hoped, federal disinvestment in the cities combined with Washington's unwillingness to bear a fair share of the social costs of mass immigration (national not local government pockets the fiscal surplus generated by newcomers) have exploded what remains of New Deal–era allegiances. The old civil rights coalition between Blacks and Latinos, first built during the progressive campaigns of the 1940s and temporarily renewed by Jesse Jackson in the 1980s, collapsed across in the country during the 1990s. As the fiscal noose has tightened around city budgets, demographically ascendant Latino communities – hungry for more control over schools, transit and public employment – have found themselves locked in increasingly bitter zero-sum conflicts with Black leaderships unwilling to share hardwon gains. (Traditional politics provides little leverage on the fabulous fiscal assets selfishly guarded by separately incorporated edge cities and outer

suburbs.) Political friction over public-sector resources, as distinguished from job competition in the private marketplace, has eroded
the dream of a rainbow coalition.

It has also opened the door to a resurgence of white political
elites in the city halls of the nation's three largest cities. With the
help of powerful Latino allies, Rudolf Giuliani (Herman Badillo),
Richard Riordan (Richard Alatorre) and Richard M. Daley (Louis
Gutierrez) have deftly exploited accumulated Latino grievances
over the failure of power-sharing during Black mayoral regimes in
the 1980s and early 1990s. Temporarily at least, they allied crucial
chunks of the Latino vote (ranging from 40 percent in New York
to 60 percent in Chicago and Los Angeles) with shrinking white
electorates to marginalize African-Americans.[247] The confiscation
of power from Blacks has been stunning and deeply embittering,
although only in Chicago, where Daley Jr. rewarded Latino supporters with key appointments and $200 million in new school
investment, has any obvious material advantage accrued to Chicanos or Puerto Ricans.[248] (Riordan, to the disappointment of his
original conservative backers, has, however, stayed scrupulously
neutral in L.A.'s recent labor wars.) Savvy conservative pundits of
both parties have applauded this realignment, reasoning that Latinos' inevitable demands will generate more conflict with Blacks
and thus become the final nail in the coffin of urban liberalism.

The worst-case scenario (and national object-lesson for pro-
gressives) is the beleagured city of Compton.[249] Since Douglas
Dollarhide became the West's first Black mayor in 1969, the city
of 100,000 has faced extraordinary obstacles in its struggle to rebuild its business and tax base after panicked white flight in the

late 1960s. Although it is surrounded by port-related warehousing and manufacturing, Compton was rebuffed in every attempt to annex new revenue sources, which were allocated by the county to white-majority cities instead. Without new income, Compton was forced to relentlessly increase the fiscal pressure on its home-owners; at the same time, the major banks cut off most home and small-business financing. High property taxes, redlining and resi-dential derelection sped an exodus of the Black middle class from the city in the late 1970s, while poverty, overcrowding, welfare dependence, illiteracy and unemployment soared. Few cities suf-fered more brutally from the Reagan/Bush cutbacks in federal aid. Absentee landlords began to convert the former city of home-owners into a rent plantation for poor Blacks and, especially, new Latino immigrants. African-American public-sector professionals, together with white cops and Latino storeowners, commuted to Compton for work but lived elsewhere: community activists, as a result, increasingly used the term "neocolonialism."

Socioeconomic decline exacerbated festering Black–Latino tensions. For years tax revenue had been drained from Compton's Latino neighborhoods with little visible return investment. Some Latino leaders publicly worried that the city (which devotes an incredible 70 percent of its general fund to "public safety") was being so thoroughly strip-mined by outsiders that there would eventually be nothing left to meet the needs of their children. This perception was only reinforced when Compton's bankrupt and scandal-ridden school system – singled out by the National Education Association as "horrible" – was taken into receivership by the state. Latino residents were also enraged by the favoritism shown politically connected developers, who have squandered millions in redevelopment loans, while a string of ordinances prohibiting outdoor sales and street-vending harassed hardworking Latinos.

In the early 1990s Pedro Pallan, a long-established businessman and community activist, implored African-American leaders to defuse the gathering crisis by sharing power on the city council. Accordingly, one of the city's younger and most outspoken Black leaders, Omar Bradley, offered to back Pallan for a council seat in 1993 if he would in turn swing Latino and Samoan voters behind Bradley's bid for the mayoralty. Latinos dutifully flocked to the polls to cast what they believed was a dual vote for Bradley and Pallan. Then, before anyone could say "multiculturalism," mayor-elect Bradley reneged on his public promise to Pallan and appointed a relatively unknown African-American to the council.

The following year, to make matters worse, local television broadcast an amateur videotape of a slightly built Latino teenager being batoned and stomped by a furious African-American Compton cop. Immediately compared to the Rodney King case, the beating of seventeen-year-old Felipe Soltero became a lightning rod for accumulated Latino grievances against Compton's Black political elite. "Have the oppressed now decided to become the oppressors?" asked Latino activists as Pallan and his followers demanded a Justice Department investigation of "discrimination" in Compton. Bradley, for his part, evinced little respect for the feelings of Latinos when, after viewing the Soltero video, he icily commented, "No reaction." Indeed, as a surging Latino population became a clear majority in the city during the second half of the 1990s, Bradley and his followers became more truculent and intransigent. The mayor, who calls Latinos "agitators," likes to quote Frederick Douglass mischievously out of context: "Power concedes nothing without demand."

African-American journalist Darryl Fears has contrasted the catastrophe of inter-ethnic relations in Compton (at least on an elite level) to its sister suburb of Inglewood, where shrewd local pols have been willing to open a few doors to the emergent Latino majority. Although there are still stark inequalities in overall representation and status, Latinos have a council seat and several high offices – unlike Compton, "where the only high-ranking Latino in city government [1998] is the water department director." Indeed, as Mayor Roosevelt Dorn told Fears, "We're making every effort to bring everyone into the program. Inglewood will not follow Compton."[250] One can only hope Dorn is sincere. Locking Latinos out of power has become a suicidal course for African-Americans. By the same token, Latino retaliation – dispossessing Blacks of their political capital – simply works to the advantage of Giuliani and other enemies of the working poor. Black and Latino unity, however imperiled, remains the fulcrum of all progressive political change.

Building Black–Latino unity is also the main challenge confronting Antonio Villaraigosa, the retiring left-Democrat Speaker of the California Assembly, as he prepares to run for mayor of Los Angeles in 2001. His ability to revitalize rainbow politics, in a contest that will be the "main event" for Latinos everywhere, depends crucially on Los Angeles's dynamic union movement. As in the 1930s and the 1960s (but perhaps even more urgently in today's post-liberal climate), substantive reform through electoral politics depends less on campaign maneuvering and bloc voting than upon resources and solidarities independently generated by struggles in neighborhoods and workplaces. Only powerful extra-electoral mobilizations, with the ability to shape agendas and discipline candidates, can ensure the representation of grassroots socioeconomic as well as ethnic-symbolic interests. Without denigrating the importance of community struggles around housing, schools, pollution, policing or public transportation – or forgetting the bitter Puerto Rican experience with the ILGWU – rank-and-file-controlled trade unionism remains the best hope for empowering urban Latino communities. Equally, if there is a renaissance of American labor close at hand, it will be a story in which Latinos, along with Blacks and other new immigrants, play a central role.

15

UPRISING OF THE MILLION

Ana Alvarado is a Salvadorean immigrant to Los Angeles. For fifteen years she made beds and scrubbed toilets in Little To-kyo's luxurious New Otani Hotel – one of the crown jewels of the thirty-year crusade to redevelop downtown Los Angeles as a corpo-rate hub of the Pacific Rim. In 1995 she was fired for supporting a union organizing drive. Suites at the New Otani (developed and owned by Kajima, the world's second largest construction conglom-erate) go for anywhere from $475 to $1800 per night, but most of the hotel's staff (70 percent Latino, 25 percent Asian) earn Motel Six wages. After repeated pleas for help from a group of pro-union work-ers, Hotel Employees and Restaurant Employees (HERE) Local 11 – led by a dynamic young Latina, Maria-Elena Durazo – launched a full-scale organizing drive in 1993. The New Otani immediately hired the most notorious unionbuster in Southern California, who held "captive audience" meetings to intimidate union sympathizers while management made orwellian threats: "A few of our employees show disrespect to managers and, over a period of time, they will be dealt with in the appropriate manner." Indeed, the hotel made work-life hell for known union supporters, who were repeatedly assigned demeaning tasks and suspended for imaginary insubordinations. It even issued an "Open letter to lawless Local 11" that childishly proclaimed, "You are disgusting."[251]

Harassment of the staff acquired ugly racial overtones. According to the New Otani's general manager, Latino workers, especially those "born in other countries," were "not yet as sophisticated perhaps as some others." Thus Mexican and Salvadorean waiters were demoted to busboys and replaced by Anglos. Japanese workers were forbidden at the cost of their jobs to fraternize with Latinos, and at one point Latinos were banned from speaking to each other in Spanish. Despite the protests of several members of the Los Angeles City Council, five of the most senior, pro-union workers, including the very popular Ana Alvarado, were fired. Future historians may someday compare the New Otani's action with Colonel Harrison Gray Otis's mass dismissal of his union printers in 1892: each was a declaration of war on labor that opened an defining era of class conflict in Los Angeles.

If New York City is reinventing Latin American culture, then metropolitan Los Angeles, with its huge Mexican/Central American working class (an estimated 500,000 factory and 1.5 million service workers), may yet reshape the American labor movement.[252] As it enters its eighth year with no sign of weakening on either side, the New Otani campaign not only remains in the forefront of the most dramatic uprising of immigrant labor since the early days of César Chávez's farmworkers, but has become an extraordinary experiment in city-wide and international solidarity. Among the workers' earliest allies, for instance, were veterans of Little Tokyo Peoples' Rights Organization, which back in the 1970s had fought to protect the neighborhood's senior citizens and small businesses against eviction by the redevelopment juggernaut that partnered Kajima with old-guard Downtown interests. Then in 1994, Local 11 researchers discovered that Chinese survivors of a 1945 massacre at one of Kajima's slave labor camps were suing the corporation for reparations. Ana Alvarado and her Little Tokyo supporters subsequently organized rallies to publicize Kajima's sinister history, and a delegation of New Otani workers went to Tokyo to meet with the aged Chinese plaintiffs (who gave them a beautifully calligraphed banner) as well as sympathetic Japanese trade unionists. Meanwhile, union researchers began to unravel the spider's web of insider connections that has allowed Kajima to dominate so much of recent public-works construction, including the Hollywood segment of the new subway, the Long Beach Aquarium, and, most notoriously, the toxic-sited Belmont Learning Center. Without the union's persistent muckracking, it is highly unlikely that the school board would ever have had to confront the Belmont scandal.

The tactical ingenuity and strategic audacity of the New Otani campaign is not unique. Over the last decade, Latino rank-and-file workers have made the Los Angeles area the major R&D center for 21st-century trade unionism. The defiant and exuberant spirit of the *huelgas* of the 1960s and early 1970s has reemerged in one

sweatshop industry and low-paid service sector after another.
("This is war!" chant minimum-wage Latina/o janitors as they
march through office suites in swank office towers in Downtown
and Beverly Hills.) Sharing equal glory with Local 11 for giving
immigrant workers the resources to fight back has been the Service Employees' "Justice for Janitors" campaign. In 1990 a peaceful,
legal march of janitors in Century City was charged by baton-
wielding police who severely injured a number of workers; public
revulsion (and a successful lawsuit) against the LAPD has made it
less fearful for workers to use direct-action tactics borrowed from
the farmworkers' and civil rights struggles.[253]

The feisty janitors were soon followed by the American Racing
Equipment strikers in 1990–91; the militant *drywalleros* in 1992
who shut down construction sites from Ventura to the Mexican
border; the Union Spas workers in Pomona in 1993; the *drywalleros,* again, with houseframers in Orange County in 1995; county
workers and thousands of Harbor area container-haulers in 1996;
hunger-striking Latino Teamsters at Price Pfister in 1996; and
food-industry workers in the successful campaigns against Mission Guerrero Tortillas in 1996–97 and Farmer John in 1998.[254] In
addition to their long siege of the New Otani, HERE also fought
a long knock-down, drag-out battle against Los Angeles's largest
private employer, the University of Southern California. This lat-
terday Trojan war began in 1995 when the wealthy university,
whose endowment includes a large part of Downtown L.A., refused to provide guarantees of job security to its veteran catering
and cleaning workers (primarily Latino immigrants) in the event
it contracts out services. After five years of grinding confronta-

tion and mass arrests, USC finally conceded after Local 11 president Durazo, who seriously endangered her health in a dramatic hunger strike joined by Latino legislators and celebrities.

With the support of immigrant rights' groups, liberationist clergy, Latino college students and other communities of color, these new-wave campaigns have overwhelmed employers with an innovative tactical repertoire that has included guerrilla theater and film, public art, a pro-labor masked and caped avenger (Mopman), trade-union *foto-novellas* in Spanish, corporate exposés, disruption of stockholders' meetings, mass civil disobedience (from sit-ins in offices to blockage of freeways), pickets in front of bosses' homes or corporate headquarters (even in Japan), community delegations, work-to-rule, union fiestas and marches, and the encirclement of city hail by hundreds of huge trucks, as well as traditional picket-lines and boycotts.[255] Equally novel has been the bilingual Los Angeles Bus Riders Union, sponsored by the Labor-Community Strategy Center, which has organized thousands of inner-city residents to successfully protest racism in public transit expenditure.[256] All of these campaigns have, in turn, drawn formidable talent from graduates of the student protests against Proposition 187 that rocked Southern California in 1994. The "best and brightest" of the second generation want to be organizers and teachers, not MBAs.[257]

This explosion of rank-and-file energy (which longshore leader Peter Olney has aptly called the "rising of the million") has moreover allowed a bloc of progressive public-employee and service-sector unions with Latino-majority or Black-and-Latino majority memberships to wrest control of the Los Angeles County Federation of Labor from conservative, white-dominated building-trades locals. The Federation's new Latino secretary-treasurer, Miguel Contreras, is, fittingly enough, a battle-scarred hero of César Chávez's Movimiento. Moreover the new-majority unions have begun to send their own militant representatives to Sacramento, including Assemblymember Gilbert Cedillo, who led the dogged fight of county workers against hospital downsizing. Some veteran political analysts, like the *L.A. Weekly*'s Harold Meyerson, see this emergent "labor-Latino alliance" as the prime-mover that will realign California politics over the next decade.[258] Certainly the victories in Los Angeles provided powerful ammunition to those inside the national AFL-CIO who successfully lobbied the Executive to endorse an amnesty for undocumented workers, a watershed in labor's claim to speak for the interests of Latino communities.

The Latino labor uprising in Los Angeles has also cemented a multi-ethnic coalition around the campaign for a metropolitan "living wage." In 1997, the Los Angeles City Council, led by veteran teacher activist Jackie Goldberg, defied Mayor Riordan to join a dozen other cities, including Milwaukee and Baltimore, in passing a "living wage" ordinance for workers under city contract.[259] No symbolic gesture, this law has helped to create a new moral framework and wage standard for organizing everywhere in the metropolis. It injects what Marx called "an alternative political economy of the working class" into the debate about the future of Los Angeles and its emergent Latino majority. (It is, in other words, a rare contemporary example of strategic politics – that is, the control of the formulation of an issue – from the left.)

Even the Chamber of Commerce is now forced to discuss solutions to the caste-like poverty that entraps so many tens of thousands of hardworking households, as union activists have hammered home the message that labor militancy is the only viable moral alternative to poverty-driven explosions of rage and frustration like the 1992 Rodney King riots.[260] They are arguing, in effect, that "post-industrial" urban economies, regardless of the dismal assessments of so many urban theorists, can be successfully restructured through collective bargaining to support living wages (if not a return to the lost paradise of postwar "Fordism"). They are also wagering that class organization in the workplace is the most powerful strategy for ensuring the representation of immigrants' socio-economic as well as cultural and linguistic rights in the new century ahead. The emerging Latino metropolis will then wear a proud union label.

NOTES

Chapter 1   Spicing the City

1. Mitchell Moss, Anthony Townsend and Emmanuel Tobier, *Immigration Is Transforming New York City*, Taub Urban Research Center, New York University, Dec. 1997, p. 1. As elsewhere, the Census Bureau significantly undercounts Latinos in New York. For example, in 1995 the Bureau estimated that Latinos were 12.4 percent of the state's population, yet researchers at Cornell were confident that the real figure was more like 15 percent (Enrique Figueroa, "The New York State Hispanic Population: A Description and Evaluation of the Mexican Descent Group," Working Paper, Dept. of Agricultural Resources and Managerial Economics, Cornell University, Ithaca, N.Y. 1998, p. 9).

2. Elias Lopez, *Major Demographic Shifts Occurring in California*, California Research Bureau Note (State Library) 6:5, Oct. 1999, p. 8.

3. Southern California Association of Governments (SCAG), *The State of the Region: Measuring Progress into the 21st Century*, Los Angeles 1999, p. 62.

4. See US Census projections reported in the *Los Angeles Times*, 15 July, 15 and 19 Sept., 17 and 20 Oct., 5 and 7 Nov., and 18 Dec. 1999. In 2040 Latinos will be almost half of California's population (48 percent) of 58.7 million while Anglos will be less than a third (31 percen, according to California Department of Finance projections (quoted in the *Los Angeles Times*, 18 Dec. 1998).

5. SCAG, ibid.

6. For Dallas/Fort Worth, see Carol Cropper, "New Turn in Power Struggle over Dallas School System," *New York Times*, 12 Oct. 1997; and Bernard Weinstein, "An Economy in Full Swing," *Urban Land*, Sept. 1998, p. 67. The Chicago population projection for

2000 is from *U.S. News*, 5 Nov. 1991.

7. State of Illinois, *Population Trends in Illinois: 1990-2020*, n.p., n.d.

8. Philadelphia's African-American population, in contrast, is steadily declining. See Bureau of the Census press release, 15 Sept. 1999.

9. Rene Rosenbaum, *Migration and Integration of Latinos into Rural Midwestern Communities: The Case of Mexicans in Adrian, Michigan*, JSRI Research Report No. 19, Julian Samora Research Institute, East Lansing, Mich., Jan. 1997, pp. 3–4.

10. See table in Thomas Exter, *Regional Markets: Volume One—Population*, Ithaca, N.Y. 1999, p. 594. Eleven out of the twenty largest metropolitan statistical areas had larger Latino than Black populations in 1995. See Bureau of the Census, *Estimates of the Population of Metropolitan Areas*, 1996.

11. Anchorage's annual Latino Festival in July provides "a strong collective voice" for the city's fastest growing population. See *Anchorage Daily News*, 28 July 1997, and *Salt Lake Tribune*, 2 June 1996. The Portland figure doesn't include an estimated 62,000 seasonal migrants from Mexico who live in the city at some point during each year.

12. Michael Brun, et al., *A Spatial Study of the Mobility of Hispanics in Illionis and the Implications for Educational Institutions*, JSRI Working Paper No. 43, Julian Samora Research Institute, East Lansing, Mich. 1998, p. 2.

13. See "Reshaping of America," a special series on Mexican migration, *Dallas Morning News*, 19 and 22 Sept. 1999; and growth data in "Hispanic Heritage Month," Census Bureau press release, 13 Sept. 1999.

14. *Los Angeles Times*, 30 Nov. 1999.

15. Interview, research staff of Culinary Workers Union, Las Vegas, Nev., April 1996.

16. National Center for Health Statistics, *Births of Hispanic Origin, 1989–1995*, Washington, D.C. 1998; and Juan Andrade, Jr. "Latinos: A Sleeping Giant?," United States Hispanic Leadership Institute, press release, 1998.

17. Kelvin Pollard and William O'Hare, *America's Racial and Ethnic Minorities*, Population Reference Bureau, Washington, D.C. 1999, p. 17.

18. Census Bureau, Population Estimates Program press release, 29 Oct. 1999. The median age of the Mexican immigrant population is only twenty-three (Bureau of Census, March 1994 CPS: Median Age of Population by Ethnicity).

19. Thaddeus Hemck, "José Most Popular Name in Texas and California," *Houston Chronicle*, 14 Jan. 1999.

20. In Sept. 1999 the Census Bureau estimated a mainland population of 31.6 million Latinos, or 11.5 percent of the national total; and 33.2 million African-Americans, or 12.1 percent (Bureau of Census, Population Estimates Program press release, 22 Oct. 1999).

21. Barbara Vobejda, "Catching a Demographic Wave," *Washington Post National Weekly Edition*, 20 July 1998; and Bureau of the Census, *Current Population Reports: Population Projections of the United States by Age, Sex, Race, and Hispanic Origin: 1995–2050* (P25-1130), Washington, D.C., pp. 1–2, 14, and 16–17.

22. Whereas Hispanics, as a census category, have both high birthrates and high immigration rates, Asians' high immigration is offset by low fertility.

23. Another twenty-five cities will probably have Latino majorities by 2000. (Data set available at http://migration.ucdavis.edu/hspn-cnus/cityhaspl.htm.) See also Elaine Allensworth and Refugio Rochin, "Ethnic Transformation in Rural California: Beyond the Immigrant Farmworker," *Rural Sociology* 63:1 (1998).

24. Some 58 percent of the US Latino population is concentrated in the cores of just nine metropolitan areas (William Frey and Kao-Lee Liaw, "Internal Migration of Foreign-Born Latinos and Asians: Are They Assimilating Geographically?," in Kavita Pandit and Suzanne Withers, eds., *Migration and Restructuring in the United States*, Lanham, Md. 1999, p. 218).

25. Southern California Association of Governments study quoted in *Los Angeles Times*, 8 March 1998.

26. Paul Starobin, "Sectional Politics," *National Journal*, 22 Feb. 1997, p. 359. See also William Frey and Kao-Lee Liaw, "Immigrant Concentration and Domestic Migrant Dispersal: Is Movement to Nonmetropolitan Areas 'White Flight'?", *Professional Geographer* 50:2 (1998), pp. 217–18 (Frey and Liaw's answer is yes).

27. Center for Media and Public Affairs study cited in *Frontera Magazine* 2 (1996). This "brown-out" also extends to the print media: in 1996 44 percent of US daily newspapers did not have a single Latino in the newsroom (Octavio Nuiry, "Press Pass," *Hispanic Magazine*, March 1997). In public television, meanwhile, funding to Latino production consortia finances less than two hours of annual programming (Chon Noriega, "April Fools," *Aztlan* 24:1 [Spring 1999], p. 2).

28. Elizabeth Martínez, *De Colores Means All of Us*, Boston 1998, p. 9. See also Joan Petersilia and Allan Abrahams, "A Profile of Those Arrested," in Mark Baldassare, ed., *The Los Angeles Riots*, Boulder, Colo. 1994, pp. 136 and 140.

29. For an invaluable Latino perspective on Southern California in the 1980s and 1990s, including the protests against Proposition 187, see Rodolfo Acuña, *Anything But Mexican: Chicanos in Contemporary Los Angeles*, London 1997.

30. Leading centers of research include Centro de Estudios Puertorriqueños (CCNY), the César Chávez Center for Chicano Studies (UCLA), the Cuban Research Institute (Florida International University), and the Center for Mexican-American Studies (University of Texas). Together with eight other university centers, they sponsor the Inter-University Program for Latino Research.

31. Cf. Pedro Caban, "The New Synthesis of Latin American and Latino Studies" in Frank Bonilla, et al., eds., *Borderless Borders: US Latinos, Latin Americans and the Paradox of Interdependence*, Philadelphia 1998; Jeffrey Belnap and Raul Fernandez, eds., *José Martí's "Our America": From National to Hemispheric Cultural Studies*, Durham, N.C. 1998; and José Saldívar, *Border Matters: Remapping American Cultural Studies*, Berkeley, Calif. 1997.

Chapter 2   Buscando América

32. Frank Bean and Marta Tienda, *The Hispanic Population of the United States*, Russell Sage Foundation, New York 1987.

33. Barbara Gutierrez, "Hispanic? Latino?," *Miami Herald*, 7 Nov. 1999.

34. Neil Foley, "Becoming Hispanic: Mexican Americans and the Faustian Pact with

Whiteness," in Foley, ed., *Reflexiones 1997: New Directions in Mexican American Studies*, Austin, Texas 1997, p.53.

35. Cf. Acuña, p. 9; Juan Flores, *Divided Borders: Essays on Puerto Rican Identity*, Houston, Texas 1993, p. 184; Suzanne Oboler, *Ethnic Labels, Latino Lives*, Minneapolis, Minn. 1995; and Geoffrey Fox, *Hispanic Nation: Culture, Politics and the Constructing of Identity*. Tucson, Ariz. 1996, pp. 12–15.

36. John Phelan, "Pan-Latinism, French Intervention in Mexico and the Genesis of the Idea of Latin America," in *Conciencia y autenticidad historias*, Mexico D.F. 1968.

37. "Beginning in the early nineteenth century French scholars constructed and nurtured a Latin identity for France. Imbued with both racial and cultural meaning, Latinity was also applied to the peoples of Southern Europe, and Spanish and Portuguese America. Coined by French and Paris-based Spanish American intellectuals in the 1850s, the term 'Latin America' itself was invented in opposition to the expansionist 'Anglo-Saxon' United States. Indeed, the Anglo threat to Latin civilization in Mexico provided Napoleon III with an ideological motive for his Mexican expedition. More generally, however, observers of modern South and Central America were guided by new racial and cultural associations. As Latin, South and Central America were understood by elites on both sides of the Atlantic as racially and culturally akin to France (the preeminent Latin power) and decisively embarking on the route to modernity. The Latin American people were viewed by the French as both Others and brothers. In effect, *Latin* America was cleansed of indigenous obstacles to progress, a clearing operation aided by the social scientific confinement of the Indian to the distant past and the scholarly spaces of the museum, archive and laboratory" (Paul Edison, *Latinizing America: The French Scientific Study of Mexico, 1830–1930*, PhD thesis, Columbia University 1999, pp. 5–6).

38. "The popular veneration of a digital photograph is as sure a sign as any of the cataclysmic shift under way in modern perception" (Christopher Knight, "Diverse Forces Remake the Seen," *Los Angeles Times Calendar*, 26 Dec. 1999, p. 68).

39. *National Catholic Reporter*, 11 Feb. 2000.

40. Carlos Monsiváis, "Dreaming of Utopia," *NACLA Report on the Americas* 19:3 (Nov./Dec. 1995), p. 41.

41. Xavier Totti, "The Making of a Latino Ethnic Identity," *Dissent*, Fall 1987, pp. 537–42.

42. Flores, p. 203.

43. Octavio Paz, "Vuelta a el laberinto de la soledad," in *El ogro filantrópico: historia y política*, Barcelona 1979, p. 17.

44. Speaking about the huge German-speaking community in Gilded Age New York, Stanley Nadel writes: "Selecting from a broad range of historically developed options, they shaped their ethnicity in accordance with whichever set of rules seemed appropriate for the particular context. Then, having molded an image out of a melange of culture, emotion, and ideology, they reified it into a seemingly timeless identity" (*Little Germany: Ethnicity, Religion, and Class in New York City, 1845–80*, Urbana, Ill. 1990, p.7).

45. On multiple and often antagonistic *mexicanidads* in El Paso/Ciudad Juárez, see Pablo Villa, *Crossing Borders, Reinforcing Borders: Social Categories, Metaphors and Narrative Identities on the US–Mexico Frontier*, Austin, Texas 2000.

46. Mano Garcia, *Mexican Americans: Leadership, Ideology and Identity, 1930–1960*, New Haven, Conn. 1989.

47. Foley, ibid.

48. Ignacio Garcia, *Chicanismo: The Forging of a Militant Ethos among Mexican Americans*, Tucson, Ariz. 1997.

49. Cf. Harley Browning and Rodolfo O. de la Garza, eds., *Mexican Immigrants and Mexican Americans: An Evolving Relation*, Austin, Texas 1986; and David Gutierrez, *Walls and Mirrors: Mexican Americans, Mexican Immigrants, and the Politics of Ethnicity*, Berkeley, Calif. 1995.

50. Rubén Martínez, *The Other Side: Fault Lines, Guerrilla Saints and the True Heart of Rock 'n' Roll*, London 1992; and Guillermo Gómez-Peña, *The New World Border*, San Francisco 1996.

51. See 1996 editorial manifesto by Yvette Doss at *Frontera Magazine* website.

52. Juan Flores's essays in *Divided Borders* are brilliant, jazz-like riffs on the struggles to reclaim Puerto Rican, Latino, and, indeed, American identities from the clutches of messianic US exceptionalism and bottom-line corporate multiculturalism. See also Ramón Grosfoguel, "Puerto Rican Labor Migration to the United States," *Review* 22:4 (1999).

53. The cases of Guadeloupe and Martinique (now, anomalously, parts of the European Union) offer rich and unexploited comparisons to the Puerto Rican dilemma. See, for example, Marie-Claude Celeste, "Songes independantistes dans les Antilles," *Le Monde Diplomatique*, Dec. 1999, p. 18.

54. "Enter Jennifer Lopez playing Selena and at last the Puerto Rican diaspora has a big *culo* to call our own, ending a long stretch of second-class citizenship in both the US and Puerto Rico" (Frances Negron-Muntener, "Jennifer's Butt," *Aztlán* 22:2 [Fall 1997], p. 191).

55. On Spanish-language media, see Fox, pp. 42–52.

56. Important cultural strands of native California – Gabrielino, Chumash, Diegueño, etc. – are also preserved in Southern California's older Chicano communities.

57. See *Latino Ethnic Consciousness: The Case of Mexican Americans and Puerto Ricans in Chicago*, South Bend, Ind. 1985, pp. 4–11; also, *Puerto Rican Chicago*, South Bend, Ind. 1987.

58. Max Castro, "The Politics of Language in Miami," in Romero, ed., p. 290.

59. On relations between Cubans and Nicaraguans, cf. Sheila Croucher, *Imagining Miami: Ethnic Politics in a Postmodern World*, Charlottesville, Va. 1997, esp. p. 51; and Patricia Fernandez-Kelly, "From Estrangement to Affinity: Dilemmas of Identity Among Hispanic Children," in Bonilla et al., p. 91.

60. *New York Times*, 28 Feb. 2000.

61. Flores, p. 183.

62. James Allen and Eugene Turner, *The Ethnic Quilt: Population Diversity in Southern California*, Northridge, Calif. 1997, p. 251. Fourteen percent, however, is a large number in absolute terms, and in 1997 (for California as a whole) "interracial" children including Latino and Anglo mixtures were the third category of births after Latinos and whites (Kevin Pollard and William O'Hare, *America's Racial and Ethnic Minorities*, Population Reference Bureau, 1999, p. 13).

63. Cf. Gabriel Haslip-Viera and Sherrie Bayer, "Introduction," in Haslip-Viera and Bayer, eds., *Latinos in New York City: Communities inTransition*, South Bend, Ind. 1996, p. xix; and Totti, p. 542.

64. Silvio Torres-Saillant, "Visions of Dominicanness in the United States," in Bonilla, et al., p. 141.

65. Flores, p. 184.

66. Ilan Stavans, *The Hispanic Condition: Reflections on Culture and Identity in America*. New York 1995, pp. 9 and 13.

67. Whereas *Newsweek* and other national media have trumpeted Rickymania etc. as the arrival of Latinos in the cultural mainstream, many Latino critics have argued that Latinos remain as marginalized as ever. They cite such examples as the absence of Latino (and Black) characters in the 1999 television season, the exclusion of Spanish-surname players (even the legendary Roberto Clemente) from Major League Baseball's All Century-Team, the Corporation for Public Broadcasting's defunding of the National Latino Communications Center, and the continuing studio preference for Anglo executives in "Latin programming."

68. Alfredo Valladao, *The Twenty-First Century Will Be American*, London 1996, pp. 48–9 and 195–6.

Chapter 3   La Frontera's Siamese Twins

69. See my "Huellas Fronterizas," *Grand Street* 56 (1996).

70. See the fascinating but sadly unpublished history by Vincent de Baca, "Moral Renovation of the Californias: Tijuana's Political and Economic Role in American–Mexican Relations, 1920–1935," PhD thesis, University of California, San Diego, 1991.

71. Up to a fifth of the populations of some northern Mexican states now resides north of the border (*Los Angeles Times*, 31 July 1998).

72. Peter Andreas, "Sovereigns and Smugglers: Enforcing the United States–Mexico Border in the Age of Economic Integration," PhD diss., Cornell University 1999, p. 12.

73. Ibid.

74. Josiah Heyman, "The Mexico–United States Border in Anthropology: A Critique and Reformulation," *Journal of Political Ecology* 1 (1994), pp. 49 and 56.

75. See Emilio Pradilla Cobo, "The Limits of the Mexican Maquiladora Industry," *Review of Radical Political Economics* 25:4 (1993), pp. 91–108; Elizabeth Fussell, "The Gendered Geography of Production: Women and Work in Tijuana and Mexico," PhD diss., University of Wisconsin, Madison, 1998.

76. Nichola Lowe and Martin Kenney, "Foreign Investment and the Global Geography of Production: Why the Mexican Consumer Electronics Industry Failed," *World Development*, 27:8 (1999), p. 1434.

77. Daniel Arreola and James Curtis at the University of Arizona have compared the distinctive spatial organizations of fourteen cities on the Mexican side of the fence: *The Mexican Border Cities: Landscape Anatomy and Place Personality*, Tucson, Ariz. 1993.

78. Population from *Demographic Atlas of San Diego/Tijuana*, 1996; and *maquiladoras* from Mexico: Secretaria de Comercio y Fomento Industrial, 1998.

79. Cf., Lawrence Herzog, *Where North Meets South: Cities, Space and Politics on the U.S-Mexico Border*, Austin, Tex. 1990; Oscar Martinez, *Border People: Life and Society in the US–Mexico Borderlands*, Tucson, Ariz. 1994; and M. Keamey and A. Knopp, *Border Cities: A History of the US–Mexican Twin Cities*, Austin, Tex. 1995.

80. "Seeking US Suppliers for Maquiladoras," *Mexico Business Monthly*, Sept. 1997.

81. Scott Grimes and Tamara Richardson, "Regional Links to Asia: What Does the Relationship Mean to San Diego and Northern Baja California?" working paper, San Diego Dialogue, June 1998, pp. 4 and 7.

82. Devon Peña, *The Terror of the Machine: Technology, Work, Gender and Ecology on the US–Mexican Border*, Austin, Tex. 1997, pp. 275–6. "Instead of adapting the Toyotist regime to cross-cultural dynamics, Japanese transnationals with Mexican *maquilas* have integrated their production strategies, in basically unmodified form, into a structure that gives management enormous leeway in the mediation and control of industrial conflicts and the micromanagement of shop-floor struggles. This is what I have called hyper-Toyotism, because it involves a strategy that exaggerates tendencies already found in the historical Japanese context" (p. 276).

83. *Demographic Atlas of San Diego/Tijuana*.

84. "*Colonias*: Problems and Promise," *BorderLines* 6:1 (Feb. 1998); and Peter Ward, *Colonias in Texas and Mexico: Urbanization by Stealth*, Austin, Tex. 1999.

85. EPA, as paraphrased by Peña, p. 291.

86. Cyrus Reed, "Hazardous Waste Management on the Border," *BorderLines* 6:5 (July 1998).

87. Heather Williams, "Mobile Capital and Transborder Labor Rights Mobilization," *Politics and Society*, 27:1 (March 1999), pp. 140–41.

88. *US Water News Online*, Nov. 1996.

89. Thomas Kelly, "Sewage Diplomacy: The Political Geography of Cross-Border Sewage Flows at San Diego-Tijuana," PhD diss., Fletcher School, 1994.

90. See David Shirk, "New Federalism in Mexico: Implications for Baja California and the Cross-Border Region," working paper, San Diego Dialogue, July 1999.

91. Timothy Dunn, *The Militarization of the US–Mexican Border, 1978–1992*, Austin, Tex. 1996. Operation Gatekeeper was modeled on El Paso's 1993 Operation Blockade and has been followed by Operation Safeguard in Nogales and Operation Rio Grande in Brownsville.

92. Peter Andreas, "Borderless Economy, Barricaded Border," *NACLA Report on the Americas* 33:3 (Nov./Dec. 1999), p. 16.

93. Andreas, *Sovereigns and Smugglers*, pp. 5–6. "Moreover the focus on border controls has obscured and drawn attention away from the more complex and politically divisive challenge of curbing the domestic US demand for both imported drugs and migrant labor" (p. 14).

94. Hector Tobar, "New Border in Tijuana," *L.A. Weekly*, 15–21 March 1996.

95. Karl Eschbach, et al., "Death at the Border," *International Migration Review* 33:2 (Summer 1999), p. 431; and Nate Seltzer, "Immigration Law Enforcement and Human Rights Abuses," *BorderLines* 6:9 (Nov. 1998).

96. Nor do they recall the ominous precedent of the 1992 Los Angeles riots when the regular military, federal police agencies (including a huge Border Patrol contingent), the national guard and local police occupied inner-city neighborhoods, often in the most brazen defiance of civil liberties.

97. Dane Schiller, "Mighty Border Patrol Force Finds Deep Ambivalence Along the Rio Grande," *New York Times News Service*, 1998.

98. Heather Williams, p. 140. See also Raul Hinojosa-Ojeda and Sherman Robinson, "Labor Issues in a North American Free Trade Area," in N. Lustig, B. Bosworth and R. Lawrence, eds., *North American Free Trade: Assessing the Impact*, Washington, D.C. 1992.

99. Moisés Sánchez Limón, "En Tijuana, 600 ejecuciones en un año, denuncian abogados," *Cronica*, 11 Jan. 1998; Sebastian Rotella, *Twilight on the Line: Underworlds and Politics at the US–Mexico Border*, New York 1998, p. 236.

100. Cf. *New York Times*, 26 Sept. 1998; *Los Angeles Times*, 2 Oct. 1998; and *San Diego Union-Tribune*, 12 Aug. 1999.

101. See Chapter 4 in Rotella, *Twilight on the Line*; and Anne Marie Mackler, "Another Girl Found Murdered," *Frontera NorteSur*, Jan. 1999.

Chapter 4   The Latino Metropolis

102. Herbert Bolton's famous *The Spanish Borderlands* (New Haven, Conn. 1921) gave Border Studies an epistemological charter, but its disciplinary development was primarily nurtured by New Mexican Charles Loomis at Michigan State (in a department notorious for its role in US counterinsurgency planning against Latin American guerrilla movements in the 1960s) and by Coloradan Julian Samora at Nortre Dame.

103. Potentially pathbreaking research is in process, however. Christopher Hansen and Angelo Falcon are currently finishing a typological analysis of Latino neighborhoods in New York, and Morgan Appel is working on a similar project in the metropolitan Los Angeles area as contributions to an ambitious five-city comparative study undertaken by the Latino Urban Policy Agenda, a consortium of four leading Latino policy centers.

104. Gregory Squires, et al., *Chicago: Race, Class and the Response to Urban Decline*, Philadelphia 1987, p. 110; and Nicholas De Genova, "Working the Borderlines, Making the Difference: Race and Space in Mexican Chicago," PhD diss., Univesity of Chicago, 1999.

105. Institute for Puerto Rican Policy, *New York City Latino Neighborhoods Databook*, New York 1996.

106. "The German-American community grew tenfold within thirty years and by 1875 encompassed one-third of New York City's population. By 1880. it had reached the size of the entire city of New York in 1845. The German New York metropolis, with over half a million people, was thus a third German capital, larger than any German city other than Berlin or Vienna" (Nadel, p. 41).

107. In a study of five key metropolitan areas – Los Angeles, San Francisco, Chicago,

Miami and New York – a team of economic geographers came to the conclusion that immigration replaced but did not displace natives. The outflow was driven by economic restructuring and the rise of edge cities, not by immigration (Richard Wright, Mark Ellis and Michael Reibel, "The Linkages Between Immigration and Internal Migration in Large Metropolitan Areas in the United States," *Economic Geography*, pp. 235–40).

108. Cf. Mike Davis, "The Empty Quarter," in David Reid, ed., *Sex, Death, and God in L.A.*, New York 1992; and Nancy Abelmann and John Lie, *Blue Dreams: Korean Americans and the Los Angeles Riots*, Cambridge, Mass. 1995, esp. pp. 137–40. The economic geography of Latino Los Angeles will be a major theme in the important forthcoming book by Victor Valle and Rudy Torres, *Latino Metropolis*.

109. On the residential and occupational geography of Guatemalans and Salvadoreans in Los Angeles, see David Lopez, Eric Popkin and Edward Telles, "Central Americans: At the Bottom, Struggling to Get Ahead," in Roger Waldinger and Medhi Bozorgmehr, eds., *Ethnic Los Angeles*, New York 1996.

Chapter 5   Tropicalizing Cold Urban Space

110. Ortiz, p. 247; Melvin Oliver and James Johnson, "Interethnic Conflict in an Urban Ghetto: The Case of Blacks and Latinos in Los Angeles," *Research in Social Movements, Conflict and Change* 6 (1984).

Chapter 6   The Third Border

111. Unless otherwise referenced, this chapter is based on Alessandra Moctezuma and Mike Davis, "Policing the Third Border," *ColorLines* 2:3 (Fall 1999); and Mike Davis, "The Social Roots of Proposition 187," *NACLA Report on the Americas* 29:3 (Nov./Dec. 1995).

112. *Chicago Sun-Times*, 8 July 1995; *Comparative Guide to American Suburbs*, 1997.

113. Paul Cuadros, "Cicero Law Blocks Latinos," *Chicago Reporter*, June 1993. By 2002, three of Chicago's older western suburbs are projected to become majority Latino: Cicero, Hodgkins and Stone Park. (See Danielle Gordon, "'White Flight' Taking Off in Chicago Suburbs," *Chicago Reporter*, Dec. 1997.)

114. Dannielle Gordon, "Chicago Area Beefs Up Its Borders,' *Chicago Reporter*, May 1998.

115. Roberto Suro, *Strangers Among Us*, New York 1998, p. 47.

Chapter 7   Fabricating the "Brown Peril"

116. This account, unless otherwise referenced, is based on my "Behind the Orange Curtain," *Nation*, 31 Oct. 1994.

117. Victor Garcia and Laura Gonzalez Martinez, *Guanajuatense and Other Mexican Immigrants in the United States: New Communities in Non-Metropolitan and Agricultural Areas*, JSRI Research Report No. 47, Julian Samora Research Institute, East Lansing, Mich. 1999, p. 2.

118. *Los Angeles Times*, 5 Feb. 1995.

Chapter 8   Transnational Suburbs

119. Miguel Szekely, "Economics of Poverty, Inequality and Wealth Accumulation in Mexico," Inter-American Development Bank study cited in *Los Angeles Times*, 7 Jan. 1999.

120. Julio Moguel, "Salinas' Failed War on Poverty," *NACLA Report on the Americas* 28:1 (July/Aug. 1994), p. 39.

121. For a summary of the changed dynamics of emigration, see Wayne Cornelius, "From Sojourners to Settlers: The Changing Profile of Mexican Immigration to the United States," in J. Bustamante, C. Reynolds and R. Hinojosa-Ojeda, eds., *US–Mexico Relations: Labor Market Interdependence*, Stanford, Calif. 1992, pp. 155–92.

122. Monsiváis, "Dreaming of Utopia," p. 39.

123. The migradollar estimate is arrived at by adding P. Martin's calculation of Mexican immigrants' annual remittances ($6–$7 billion) to commonly quoted figures for the repatriated money flow to Central America ($2–$3 billion). See P. Martin, "Mexico, Polls, Remittances and Economy," *Migration News*, Oct. 1996; and Luis Guarnizo, "Los Dominicanyorks: The Making of a Binational Society," in Romero, et al., p. 166.

124. Dennis Conway and Jeffrey Cohen, "Consequences of Migration and Remittances for Mexican Transnational Communities," *Economic Geography* 74:1 (Jan. 1998), pp. 26–44.

125. Cf. R. Alarcon, "Nortenización: Self-Perpetuating Migration from a Mexican Town," in J. Bustamante, et al., eds., *US–Mexican Relations*, pp. 302–18; and N. Glick-Schiller, L. Basch and C. Blanc-Szanton, "From Immigrant to Transmigrant: Theorizing Transnational Migration," *Anthropological Ouarterley* 68:1 (1995), pp. 131–40.

126. Roger Rouse, "Mexican Migration and the Social Space of Postmodernism," *Diaspora* 1:1 (Spring 1991), p. 14.

127. Pen Fletcher, "La Casa de Mis Sueños: Migration and Houses in a Transnational Mexican Community," PhD diss., Johns Hopkins University, 1996, p. 4.

128. Suro, pp. 32–3 and 45.

129. Ibid. pp. 33–4.

130. Robert Smith, "Transnational Migration, Assimilation, and Political Community," in Margaret Graham and Alberto Vourvolias-Bush, eds., *The City and the World: New York's Global Future*, New York 1997, p. 119. See also his "Mixteca in New York: New York in Mixteca," *NACLA Report on the Americas* 26:1 (1992).

131. See Sam Quinones and Alan Mittelstaedt, "A League of Their Own: How a Team of Oaxacan Busboys Is Redefining L.A. Basketball," *L.A. Weekly*, 4 Feb. 2000.

132. Cf. Smith, "Transnational Migration," pp. 117–19; and his "Mexicans in New York" in Haslip-Viera and Bayer, eds., pp. 67–9, 77 and 79.

133. Nancy Cleeland, "A Mexican State's Crowning Glory," *Los Angeles Times*, 20 Nov. 1999.

134. Michael Jones-Correa, *Between Two Nations: The Political Predicament of Latinos in New York City*, Ithaca, N.Y. 1998, pp. 128–9 and 164–5. See also the important study by Eugenia Georges, *The Making of a Transnational Community: Migration, Development, and Cultural Change in the Dominican Republic*, New York 1990.

135. "The New Immigrant Tide: A Shuttle Between Worlds," three-part series, *New York Times*, 19 July 1998.

136. Cf., Sam Dillon, "Mexico Considers Extending Presidential Vote to Immigrants in USA," *New York Times New Service*, 1998.

137. *Los Angeles Times*, 25 March 1998.

138. For the historical background of immigrant networks and labor organization in California, see Devra Weber, "Historical Perspectives on Transnational Mexican Workers in California," in John Hart, ed., *Border Crossings: Mexican and Mexican-American Workers*, Wilmington, Del. 1998.

139. Sarah Mahier, *American Dreaming: Immigrant Life on the Margins*, Princeton, N.J. 1995, p. 21.

140. Cf. Carol Zabin, "Organizing Latino Workers in the Los Angeles Manufacturing Sector: The Case of American Racing Equipment Company," unpublished research paper, U.C. Berkeley Labor Center, 1998; Ruth Milkman and Kent Wong, "The 1992 Southern California Drywall Strike," conference paper, "Immigrants and Union Organizing in California," May 1998; and David Bacon, *Unions and the Upsurge of Immigrant Workers*, Northern California Coalition for Immigrant Rights, n.p., n.d.

141. Diana Marcum, "The Busboys of San Miguel," *Los Angeles Times Magazine*, 14 Dec. 1997.

142. Robert Rouse, "Mexican Migration," in David Guiterrez, ed., *Between Two Worlds, Mexican Immigrants in the United States*, Wilmington, Del. 1996, p. 253.

143. Maria de los Angeles Crummell, "Gender, Class and Households," in Adela de la Tone and Beatriz Pesquera, eds., *Building with Our Hands: New Directions in Chicana Studies*, Berkeley, Calif. 1993, pp. 162–4. Also see Dennis Conway and Jeffrey Cohen, "Consequences of Migration and Remittances for Mexican Transnational Communities," *Economic Geography* 74:1 (Jan. 1998).

144. Fletcher, pp. 10–11 and 169.

145. Recent pathbreaking studies of the gendered social structures of immigration include Donna Gabbacia, *From the Other Side: Women, Gender, and Immigrant Life in the US, 1820–1990*, Bloomington, Ind. 1994; and Pierrette Hondagneu-Sotelo, *Gendered Transitions: Mexican Experiences of Immigration*, Berkeley, Calif. 1994.

146. Ramona Hernandez and Silvio Torres-Saillant, "Dominicans in New York: Men, Women, and Prospects," in Haslip-Viera and Baver, eds., p. 43. A contrasting view is offered by Karin Weyland, "Dominican Women 'Con un pie aquí y el otro allá': International Migration, Class, Gender and Cultural Change," PhD diss., New School for Social Research 1999.

147. Cf. Sherri Grasmuck and Ramon Grosfoguel, "Geopolitics, Economic Niches, and Gendered Social Capital Among Recent Caribbean Immigrants to New York City," *Sociological Perspective* 40:3 (1997), pp. 343–53; and Jacqueline Hagan, "Social Networks, Gender, and Immigrant Incorporation: Resources and Constraints," *American Sociological Review*, 63 (Feb. 1998), pp. 57–9. See also Greta Gilbertson, "Women's Labor and Enclave Employment: The Case of Dominican and Colombian Women in New York City," *International Migration Review* 29 (1995).

Chapter 9   Falling Down

148. *New York Times*, 24 Nov. 1999.

149. Ibid.

150. *New York Times*, 1 Feb. 2000.

151. Smith, "Mexicans in New York," pp. 63–4.

152. Jack Miles, "Blacks vs. Browns," *Atlantic Monthly*, Oct. 1992. Miles cites as his authority Melvin Oliver and James Johnson, "Interethnic Conflict in an Urban Ghetto: The Case of Blacks and Latinos in Los Angeles," *Research in Social Movements, Conflict and Change* 6 (1984).

153. See R. Lalonde and R. Topel, "The Assimilation of Immigrants in the US Labor Market," in G. Borjas and R. Freeman, eds., *Immigration and the Workforce*, Chicago 1992.

154. Mark Ellis and Richard Wright, "The Industrial Division of Labor Among Immigrants and Internal Migrants to the Los Angeles Economy," *International Migration Review* 33:1 (Spring 1999), p. 50.

155. Richard Wright, Mark Ellis, and Michael Reibel, "The Linkage Between Immigration and Internal Migration in Large Metropolitan Areas in the United States," *Economic Geography*, pp. 235–7.

156. Kevin McCarthy and Georges Vernez, *Immigration in a Changing Economy: California's Experience: Questions and Answers*, RAND Center for Research on Immigration Policy, Santa Monica, Calif. 1998, pp. 36–7 and 39.

157. D. Massey and N. Denton, *American Apartheid: Segregation and the Making of the Underclass*, Cambridge, Mass. 1993.

158. "The New Americans" discussed in John Maggs, "The Economics of Being Hispanic," *National Journal*, 14 Aug. 1999, p. 2361.

159. Vilma Ortiz, "The Mexican-Origin Population: Permanent Working Class or Emerging Middle Class?" in Waldinger and Bozorgmehr, p. 257.

160. Ibid.

161. Ortiz, p. 250; and Robert Waldinger, "Ethnicity and Opportunity in the Plural City," in Waldinger and Bozorgmehr, p. 451.

162. Ellis and Wright (1999), p. 49.

163. McCarthy and Vernez, p. 23: 85 percent of the 6.9 million new jobs created in the California economy between 1970 and 1990 were occupied by workers with some college education.

164. Elias Lopez, Enrique Ramirez and Refugio Rochin, *Latinos and Economic Development in California*, California Research Bureau, Sacramento, Calif. 1999, p. 7.

165. Dillon, p. 126.

166. María De los Angeles Torres, "Working Against the Miami Myth," *Nation*, 24 Oct. 1988, p. 393.

167. Census Bureau, "Disparity Between Hispanics, Whites Increases," press release, Washington, D.C. 1997.

168. Calculated from *Monthly Labor Review* data for 1990 and 1995.

169. Since 1997, however, the economy's insatiable demand for labor has begun to sub-stantially redress the losses of the early 1990s. The poverty rate for Latino children, for instance, fell from its historic 1994 high of 41.5 percent to 34.4 percent in 1998. See "In-creases in Income and Declines in Poverty," press release, National Council of La Raza, 30 Sept. 1999.

170. *Los Angeles Times*, 18 Dec. 1998. See, for example, Eric Toder and Sandeep Solanki, *Effects of Demographic Trends on Labor Supply and Living Standards*, Urban Institute, Wash-ington, D.C. 1999.

171. Maggs, p. 2361.

172. Ibid., p. 2359.

173. Marcelo Siles, *Income Differentials in the US: Impact on Latino Socio-Economic Develop-ment*, JSRI Working Paper No. 33, Julian Samora Research Institute, East Lansing, Mich. 1997, p. 9.

174. James Allen and Eugene Turner, *The Ethnic Quilt: Population Diversity in Southern California*, Berkeley, Calif. 1997, p. 173.

175. Rebecca Morales and Paul Ong, "The Illusion of Progress: Latinos in Los Angeles," in Rebecca Morales and Frank Bonillo, eds., *Latinos in a Changing US Economy*, Newbury Park, Calif. 1993, p. 74.

176. *Online NewsHour Forum*, "The Declining Economic Power of Hispanics," 21 Feb. 1997.

177. Edwin Melendez, "Hispanics and Wage Inequality in New York City," in Haslip-Viera and Bayer, eds., pp. 191 and 197.

178. In a 1980 study, native-born (34 percent clerical and 17 percent factory) and immi-grant Latinas (37 percent factory and 16 percent clerical) were represented in manufactur-ing and clerical office markets in almost inverse proportions (Dowel Myers and Cynthia Cranford, "Temporal Differentiation in the Occupational Mobility of Immigrant and Na-tive-born Latina Workers," *American Sociological Review* 63 [Feb. 1998], p. 70).

179. "The Digital Divide," *San Francisco Chronicle*, May 4, 1998.

180. *Los Angeles Times*, 20 Jan. 2000.

181. Pollard and O'Hare, p. 38.

Chapter 10   The Puerto Rican Tragedy

182. "Gary Burtless, an economist at the Brookings Institution ... says he tends to think that the disadvantages Hispanics face – even after several generations in the United States – will diminish over time. The United States, almost alone among developed nations, confers one advantage that tends to reduce the disadvantages faced by immigrant groups – full citizenship for anyone born here" (Maggs, p. 2361).

183. Clara Rodriguez, "A Summary of Puerto Rican Migration to the United States," in Romero et al., eds., p. 106–80

184. Maria Canabal, *Poverty Among Puerto Ricans in the United States*, JSRI Working Paper No. 32, Julian Samora Research Institute, East Lansing, Mich. 1997 p. 2.

185. Cited in Canabal. See also Andres Torres and Frank Bonilla, "Decline Within the Decline: The New York Perspective," in Morales and Bonilla.

186. Francisco Rivera-Batiz and Carlos Santiago, *Island Paradox: Puerto Rico in the 1990s*, New York 1996, pp. 6, 10–14 and 78.

187. Statistics from Congreso (719 W. Girard Ave., Philadelphia, PA 19123), 1999.

188. Suro, p. 143; Task Force on the New York State Dropout Problem (1986) cited in Jesse Vasquez, "Education and Community: Puerto Ricans and Other Latinos in the Schools and Universities," in Haslip-Viera and Bayer, eds., pp. 216 and 240; *New York Times*, 28 Feb., 2000.

189. Canabal, p. 2.

190. Edwin Melendez, "Hispanics and Wage Inequality in New York City," in Haslip-Viera and Vaver, eds., p. 190.

191. Canabal, p. 2.

192. Suro, p. 148.

193. Grasmuck and Grosfoguel, pp. 346 and 348.

194. Jose Sanchez, "Puerto Rican Politics in New York: Beyond 'Secondhand' Theory," in Haslip-Viera and Bayer, eds., p. 273. The Liberal Party was an anticommunist secession, engineered by Dubinsky, from East Harlem congressman Vito Marcantonio's American Labor Party, which, until its demise in 1954, had an excellent record of sponsoring Puerto Rican leadership.

195. See the conclusions in William Clark, "Mass Migration and Local Outcomes: Is International Migration to the United States Creating a New Urban Underclass," *Urban Studies* 35:3 (1998), p. 380.

196. Ramona Hernandez, Francisco Rivera-Batiz and Roberta Godini, *Dominican New Yorkers: A Socioeconomic Profile, 1990*, Institute for Urban and Minority Education, Columbia University, New York 1995.

197. *New York Times*, 28 July 1997.

198. Mahler, p. 3.

199. Ibid.

200. *New York Times*, 21 Nov. 1999.

201. David Bacon, "INS Declares War on Labor," *Nation*, 25 Oct. 1999.

Chapter 11   Education Ground Zero

202. Figures for 1994: US Department of Education, Hispanic Dropout Project, *Final Report: No More Excuses*, Washington, D.C. 1997.

203. Andres Torres and Lisa Chavez, *Latinos in Massachusetts: An Update*, Mauricio Gaston Institute, Boston 1998, p. 1.

204. *Los Angeles Times*, 19 Aug. 1999; Task Force on the New York State Dropout Problem (1986) cited in Vazquez, "Education and Community," in Haslip-Viera and Bayer, eds., p. 216.

205. Vazquez, pp. 240 and 242.

206. Cited in Mexican-American Studies and Research Center (University of Arizona), *The Arizona Report* 3:1 (Winter 1999).

207. Cf., Heather Knight, "Graduation Rates Rise for Blacks, Whites, Not Latinos," *Los Angeles Times*, Aug. 1997; "Hispanics Statistics," Department of Health and Human Services, March 1998; and National Center for Educational Statistics, "Dropout Rates in the United States: 1995," NCES 97-473, July 1997.

208. National Council of La Raza, "Hispanics Severely Underrepresented in Military," press release, 20 Jan. 1999.

209. California is one of only four states that requires a two-thirds majority to approve local school bonds. As a result, half of the bond issues on the ballot don't pass despite having received a majority of votes. More often than not, geriatric "empty nest" white households (together with private school families) are the principal opponents of school expenditure.

210. Cited in *Los Angeles Times* (Orange County edition), 12 June 1999.

211. Public Policy Institute of California, "Has School Finance Reform Been Good to California?" Research Brief No. 30 (Feb. 2000), p. 1.

212. *Education Week* 18:17, pp. 13, 154 and 165.

213. Public Policy Institute of California, "School Resources and Student Achievement in California," Research Brief No. 29 (Feb. 2000), p. 1–4.

214. Patrick Shields, et al., *The Status of the Teaching Profession: Research Findings and Policy Recommendations*, The Center for the Future of Teaching and Learning, Santa Cruz, Calif. 1999, p. 2. See also Ann Bradley, "Quality Crisis Seen in California Teaching Ranks," *Education Week*, 8 Dec. 1999.

215. *Los Angeles Times*, 1 Dec. (study) and 8 Dec. 1999 (qualifications).

216. *Los Angeles Times*, 8 Dec. 1999.

Chapter 12 Disabling Spanish

217. Important exceptions were the post–Pearl Harbor hysteria against Japanese-language schools in Hawai'i as well as sporadic backlashes (often tinged with upstate anti-papism) against Cajun French in southern Louisiana.

218. Castro, p. 287.

219. Quoted in PBS's *NewsHour* forum on bilingual education, 29 Sept. 1997 (see website archive).

220. She flays the Mexican American Legal Defense and Education Fund ("created, in fact, not by Hispanics but by wealthy East Coast limousine liberals") for attempting to sabotage the implementation of Proposition 227 (Jill Stewart, "Manipulative Power-Trippers." *New Times* [Los Angeles], 2 Dec. 1999). Earlier (and equally seedy) allegations by Peter Skerry in *Mexican-Americans: The Ambivalent Minority* about Chicano pols' manipulation of ethnic victimization were awarded a book prize by the *Los Angeles Times* in 1993.

221. Stephen Krashen, *Condemned Without a Trial: Bogus Arguments Against Bilingual Education*, Portsmouth, N.H. 1999, p. 49.

222. Ibid.

223. C. Rossell and K. Baker, "The Educational Effectiveness of Bilingual Education," *Research in the Teaching of English* 30:1 (1996); Patricia de Cos, *Educating California's Immigrant Children: An Overview of Bilingual Education,* California Research Bureau (State Library), Sacramento, Calif. 1999, p. 46.

224. Diane Aug. and Kenji Hakuta, eds., *Improving Schooling for Language-Minority Students: A Research Agenda,* National Academy of Sciences, Washington, D.C. 1997.

225. J. Ramirez, et al., *Final Report: Longitudinal Study of Structured English Immersion Strategy, Early-Exit, and Late-Exit Transitional Bilingual Education Programs for Language-Minority Children,* US Department of Education (300-87-0156), Washington D.C. 1991, p. 48.

226. See discussion in Luis Moll, "Multilingual Classroom Studies and Community Analysis: Some Recent Trends," *Educational Researcher* 21 (March 1992), pp. 20–24.

227. Alicia Rodriguez, "Latino Education, Latino Movement," *Educational Theory* 49:3 (Summer 1999), p. 389.

228. Tamara Lucas, Rosemary Henze and Ruben Donato, "Promoting the Success of Latino Language-Minority Students: An Exploratory Study of Six High Schools," in Antonia Darder, et al., eds., *Latinos and Education,* New York 1999, pp. 379–94

229. de Cos, *Educating Immigrant Children,* p. 27.

230. Wayne Thomas and Virginia Collier, "Accelerated Schooling for English Language Learners," *Educational Leadership,* April 1999, pp. 46–9.

231. Russell Gersten, "The Changing Face of Bilingual Education," *Education Leadership,* April 1999, p. 44.

232. Dr. Juan Andrade, press release, United States Hispanic Leadership Institute, Washington, D.C., 1 Oct. 1998.

Chapter 13   Who Will Feed the Dragon?

233. Cf., *Los Angeles Times,* 2 Feb. 1998; and Clifford Levy, "New York City's Hispanic Voters Emerge as Powerful and Unpredictable Force," *New York Times,* 8 Nov. 1997.

234. Barry Shlachter, "Public Caught in Dallas Schools' Meltdown,' *Fort Worth Star-Telegram,* 23 Sept. 1997.

235. Mike Davis, "California Uber Alles?," *CovertAction* 52 (Spring 1995); and "The Social Roots of Proposition 187," *NACLA Report on the Americas* (Nov./Dec.) 1995.

236. *Los Angeles Times,* 1 Jan. 1998.

237. *Los Angeles Times,* 8 Nov. 1996.

238. Cf. Levy; and William Schneider, "Shattering an Urban Liberal Coalition," *National Journal,* 19 April 1997, p. 790.

239. Maurillo Virgil, "Hispanics and the 1996 Presidential Election," *Latino Studies Journal* 9:1 (Winter 1998), p. 57.

240. Dick Kirschten, "Hispanics: Beyond the Myths," *National Journal,* 14 Aug. 1999, p. 2351.

241. Exit pools discussed in "Notebook," *New Republic,* 27 Dec. 1999, p. 10.

242. Kirschten, p. 2356. Figures for the Latino electorate differ.

243. Mike Davis, "Who Killed Los Angeles? Part One," *New Left Review* 197 (Jan./Feb. 1993).

244. Cf. Davis, "The Empty Quarter;" and forthcoming book by Valle and Torres.

245. Howard Blume, "The Belmont Decision," 19 Nov. 1999; and "Belmont Bungling," *L.A. Weekly*, 17 Dec. 1999.

246. See *Los Angeles Times* (Valley edition), 6 Nov. 1999.

Chapter 14   Broken Rainbows

247. See John Betancur and Douglas Gills, "Black and Latino Political Conflict in Chicago"; and William Sales and Roderick Bush, "Black and Latino Coalitions: Prospects for New Social Movements in New York City," in James Jennings, ed., *Race and Politics: New Challenges and Responses for Black Activism*, London 1997; also William Schenieder, "Shattering an Urban Liberal Coalition," *National Journal*, 19 April 1997; and Mike Davis, "The Strange Death of Liberal Los Angeles," *Z Magazine*, Nov. 1993.

248. Alysia Tate, "Gutierrez Alliance Made Daley the Latino Choice," *The Chicago Reporter*, Feb. 1999.

249. What follows is based on my "The Sky Falls on Compton," *Nation*, 19 Sept. 1994.

250. Fears, "Compton Latinos."

Chapter 15   Uprising of the Million

251. This account is based on interviews with New Otani workers and Local 11 staff; see my "Kajima's Throne of Blood," *Nation*, 12 Feb. 1996.

252. C.f., David Bacon, "Putting L.A. on the Map," *Village Voice*, 19 March 1996; and Goetz Wolff, "The Making of a Third World City?: Latino Labor and the Restructuring of the L.A. Economy," paper presented to the 17th International Congress of the Latin American Studies Association, Los Angeles, Sept. 1992.

253. Catherine Fisk, Daniel Mitchell and Christopher Erickson, "Union Representation of Immigrant Janitors in Southern California," conference paper, "Immigrants and Union Organizing in California," May 1998.

254. The labor journalist David Bacon has written scores of insightful articles covering both the labor upsurge in Southern California and the first stirrings of independent unionism in the border *maquiladoras*. In addition, see Hector Delgado, *New Immigrants, Old Unions: Organizing Undocumented Workers in Los Angeles*, Philadelphia 1993; "The Los Angeles Manufacturing Action Project: Lessons Learned, an Opportunity Squandered?" (about an organizing campaign at a tortilla company); Jose Vadi, "From 'Scabs' to Pathfinders: Militant Latino Workers in Southern California and Global Economic Restructuring," paper presented to Western Social Science Association, Albuquerque, N.M., April 1994; SEIU, *A Penny for Justice: Janitors and L.A.'s Commercial Real Estate Market*, Los Angeles 1995; and Mike Davis, "Trojan Fortress," (on the struggle at USC), *L.A. Weekly*, 1 Dec. 1995.

255. Rachel Sherman and Kim Voss, "New Organizing Tactics and Immigrant Workers,"

conference paper, "Immigrants and Union Organizing in California," May 1998.

256. Mike Davis, "Runaway Train Crushes Buses," *Nation*, 18 Sept. 1995.

257. This generation is rapidly finding its voice. See, for example, the stirring memoir by new immigrant Julian Camacho, raised in barrio Lennox near LAX, chronicling his political awakening in the late 1980s and early 1990s as a labor activist and teacher: *Growing Up Not Knowing Your Are Chicano*, Albuquerque, New Mexico 2000.

258. Harold Meyerson, "Rolling the Union On," *Dissent* (Winter 2000), p. 52.

259. Chicago Institute on Urban Poverty, *The Living Wage: In the Public Interest*, Chicago 1996.

260. For an eloquent perspective, see Edna Bonacich and Richard Appelbaum, *Behind the Label: Inequality in the Los Angeles Apparel Industry*, Berkeley, Calif. 2000.

INDEX

THE HAYMARKET SERIES

Editors: *Mike Davis and Michael Sprinker (1950–1999)*

The Haymarket Series offers original studies in politics, history and culture with a focus on North America. Representing different views across the American left on a wide range of subjects, the series will be of interest to socialists both in the USA and throughout the world. A century after the first May Day, the American left remains in the shadow of those martyrs whom the Haymarket Series honors and commemorates. These studies testify to the living legacy of political activism and commitment for which they gave their lives.

Related Titles: Published and Forthcoming

ANYTHING BUT MEXICAN: Chicanos in Contemporary Los Angeles *by Rodolfo Acuña*

THE INVENTION OF THE WHITE RACE, VOLUME I: Racial Oppression and Social Control *by Theodore Allen*

THE INVENTION OF THE WHITE RACE, VOLUME II: The Origin of Racial Oppression in Anglo-America *by Theodore Allen*

LABOR AND THE COURSE OF AMERICAN DEMOCRACY: US History in Latin American Perspective *by Charles Bergquist*

MIAMI *by John Beverley and David Houston*

IT'S NOT ABOUT A SALARY: Rap, Race and Resistance in Los Angeles *by Brian Cross, with additional text by Reagan Kelly and T-Love*

CITY OF QUARTZ: Excavating the Future in Los Angeles *by Mike Davis*

PRISONERS OF THE AMERICAN DREAM: Politics and Economy in the History of the US Working Class *by Mike Davis*

THE ASSASSINATION OF NEW YORK *by Robert Fitch*

NO CRYSTAL STAIR: African Americans in the City of Angels *by Lynell George*

WHERE THE BOYS ARE: Cuba, Cold War America and the Making of a New Left *by Van Gosse*

RACE, POLITICS AND ECONOMIC DEVELOPMENT: Community Perspectives *edited by James Jennings*

RACE AND POLITICS IN THE UNITED STATES: New Challenges and Responses to Black Activism *edited by James Jennings*